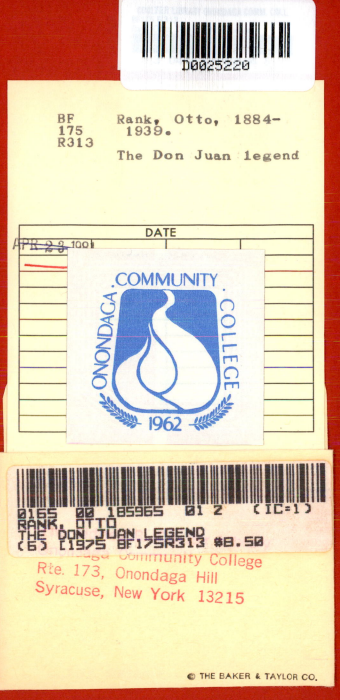

THE DON JUAN LEGEND

THE DON JUAN LEGEND

by Otto Rank, 1884-1939

*Translated and Edited, with
an Introduction by*
DAVID G. WINTER

PRINCETON UNIVERSITY PRESS
PRINCETON, NEW JERSEY

Library of Congress Cataloging in Publication Data will
be found on the last printed page of this book

Publication of this book has been aided by a grant
from the Whitney Darrow Publication Reserve Fund of
Princeton University Press

This book has been composed in Linotype Janson

Printed in the United States of America
by Princeton University Press, Princeton, New Jersey

TABLE OF CONTENTS

PREFACE

Otto Rank is today a curious and contradictory figure in the history of psychology. Acknowledged at one time as one of the most important figures in the psychoanalytic movement and the heir apparent to Freud himself, he is now not even a familiar name to the average graduate student in psychology. His early work on myth and legend displayed a brilliance of interpretation and depth of erudition that were widely acclaimed; yet many of these works are now preserved only in aging and un-translated books. His later theories of art and the artist have had some influence on theories of art; and his ideas and practices concerning psychotherapy had some influence on therapy and on different schools of the movement that is nowadays known as "humanistic psychology," though from citations and acknowledgments it is difficult to establish the precise extent of such influence. The reason for this contradiction is of course Rank's separation from psychoanalysis and Freud during the middle years of his life. Whatever may be one's view of the reasons for this separation—and a definitive assessment would surely have to wait upon a complete biography of Rank—it remains clear that the separation was the turning point in his life and work. My purpose in translating this book is, therefore, twofold: first, to make one of Rank's heretofore neglected interpretations of an important literary theme available to the present day English-speaking scholar; and second, to suggest that Rank's interpretation of the Don Juan legend, as well as the progressive changes that he made in different versions of that interpretation, may reveal some of the personal issues that were at stake in his separation from Freud, as well as in his life and work as a whole.

I first discovered Rank's book on the Don Juan legend while teaching a course at Wesleyan University on the psychological aspects of the Don Juan myth. Fragments of the present book were available in anthologies, or were cited by literary scholars; but when I read the complete original German version, I realized that these fragments and references were misleading in that they were drawn mainly from the first four chapters of the book. Shortly thereafter, I studied the Don Juan legend further in the course of working out a theory of the origins of the power motive.[1] Again, the complete text of Rank's interpretation was most valuable, as it seemed to coincide at many points with my own empirical results and ideas. Since Rank's full interpretation is not readily available even in German, I thought that an English translation would be useful. At the same time, elucidation of the connection between Rank's interpretation of Don Juan and the themes of his life might prove helpful for our understanding of Rank and his separation from Freud. Hence the rather extended biographical and analytic introduction.

Because I am interested primarily in the psychoanalytic version of Rank's work, I have used the 1924 book edition of *Die Don Juan-Gestalt* as the basis for this translation. In text footnotes and in the introduction I discuss earlier and later alterations, both major changes and minor variations. To the text I have added footnotes in brackets to suggest Rank's sources and to discuss some of the more esoteric mythic and literary examples that he used. Throughout I have used the American Psycho-

[1] See Winter (1973, Chapter 6): "The Don Juan Figure as an Archetype of the Power Motive."

logical Association convention with respect to bibliographic citations. Apart from these changes, the chapter titles and some minor corrections of Rank's own quotations, anything in the text that is my own addition, and hence responsibility, is enclosed in brackets. While I have tried to produce a readable English version of what Rank wrote, I have also tried to keep close to the original wording and style, especially where this seemed important as the basis of the arguments in the introduction. The reader should in any case be aware that Rank's writing does not always evidence a clear organization: even Freud remarked in 1906 that Rank did not always stay within the limits of his subject nor follow an outline clearly! (Nunberg and Federn, 1962, p. 10)

I am grateful for the contribution of Abigail Stewart, who discussed, suggested, and argued the interpretations given in the introduction and many issues concerning the translation, and who also encouraged the project. Others who were helpful include: Kenneth Lohf and the librarians at the Manuscript Collections and Archives Reading Room of the Columbia University Library, Carol Orr of Princeton University Press, and Harry Tucker, Jr. A fellowship from the John Simon Guggenheim Memorial Foundation supported the initial stages of the work.

LIST OF VERSIONS OF
DIE DON JUAN-GESTALT

THE ANNOTATED list which follows gives the different versions of Rank's interpretation of the Don Juan legend. In the introduction and the text itself, versions are referred to by the italicized capital letter used in this list.

A A paper given at the Vienna Psychoanalytic Association on April 26, 1922. No record of this survives, except insofar as it is identical with the manuscript of *B*, which is preserved in the Rank papers at the Columbia University Library.

B An article in *Imago*, 1922, volume 8, pages 142-96. Corrected proofs of this article are in the Rank papers. An English abstract of the article, by Louise Brink, was published in *The Psychoanalytic Review*, 1926, volume 13, pages 480-84. An English translation of excerpts from parts 1-4 (Chapters 1-4 of this book), by Walter Bodlander, appears in *The Theatre of Don Juan* (Mandel, 1963, pages 625-34).

C A book version of *Die Don Juan-Gestalt* was published by the Internationaler Psychoanalytischer Verlag in 1924. It is virtually identical to *B*, except for some minor alterations and additions. It is the basis for the present translation.

D A slightly modified version of Chapters 2-4 of the present book appeared in the *Almanach für das Jahr 1927* (Psychoanalytic almanac for 1927), published by the Internationaler Psychoanalytischer

Verlag, pages 172-80. The excerpt is titled "Don Juan and Leporello."

E   In his 1930 book *Seelenglaube und Psychologie*, Rank refers to the Don Juan legend (pages 53-62); although he cites version *C*, the interpretation is clearly quite different from *C*: it is not at all psycho-analytic, and anticipates version *F*.

F   Rank completely rewrote the book and combined it with a major revision of his book on the double motif (Rank, 1914) in a 1932 French book titled *Don Juan: Une Étude sur le Double*. The book was written in German, translated by S. Lautman, and published by Denoël and Steele.

G   A typescript, apparently of an English translation of *F*, exists in the Rank papers. Rank himself did not make the translation, but there is evidence that he reviewed it. There is no date, but from internal bibliographic evidence it was written at least in 1934 or later. While it may have been intended for publication, it never appeared. In the present trans-lation, this version has been used for occasional clarification of detail and references. Some of the major differences between *G* (thus *F*) and *C* are discussed in the introduction.

THE DON JUAN LEGEND

INTRODUCTION

THE LIFE AND WORK OF OTTO RANK

Otto Rank was one of the most brilliant and imaginative, yet surely one of the most perplexing members of the group who were drawn to Freud and who participated in the early development of psychoanalysis. Rank analyzed myth and legend with an insight and a facility that approached that of the master; his energy and resourcefulness were essential to the survival of the early psychoanalytic publishing ventures; his wide reading and knowledge of literature were more than once of assistance to Freud's own work; and he was perhaps Freud's closest continuing associate for fifteen years. Yet in the midst of his brilliant career he left the psychoanalytic movement, physically removed himself from Vienna to Paris and later New York, and in time came to disavow the principal tenets of psychoanalysis. In this later period of his life, he abandoned further analysis of myth and legend (although he continually reworked his earlier formulations), and wrote largely about the process of therapy, out of which he finally developed a world-view that is both wide-ranging and, to many readers, incompletely articulated and confusing (Rank, 1941).

Whether such a great change is interpreted as "failing mental integration," the result of a manic-depressive neurosis (Jones, 1955-57, III, Chapter 2 *passim*), or as a prolonged struggle for growth and responsible individualization (Taft, 1958, p. 98 and *passim*) is a question that must await a definitive biography of Rank, and as such is beyond the scope of this introduction. Yet *The Don Juan Legend* is important not only in its own right, but

also because it was the last work of Rank's first period—
the last analysis of a legend carried out within a psychoanalytic framework. Moreover, Rank revised the work
several times; in minor but significant ways during the
last years with Freud, and in a major way several years
after the break. Thus it will be appropriate to give some
established biographical details in order to indicate the
position of this book in Rank's life and work.

When Rank was born in Vienna in April 1884,[1] he
had a brother, Paul, who was three years older, and a
sister who later died when Rank was very young. The
family were middle class, perhaps precariously so; in any
case his family background was of a "distinctly lower
social stratum" from that of Freud's other early associates (Jones, II, p. 181). His surname at birth was
Rosenfeld; the name Rank was used first as a pen name
and then made legal in 1909 (Taft, p. 4). In his autobiography, written in 1903 as a part of his early diaries,
Rank describes his father as a "quiet drinker" who none-
theless was not "quiet after drinking"; later he compares
his father with the character Hjalmar Ekdal in Ibsen's
The Wild Duck. That apart, references to his family in
the published parts of his autobiography (in Taft) are
rather laconic, giving the general impression of parental
disinterest, punctuated by episodes of loud rage. Although the family were Jewish, they appear not to have
carried their religion beyond the observance of one or
two holy days each year.

Perhaps because of the limited family resources, as
well as a family emphasis on sons' earning their own way,

[1] This account is drawn largely from Taft (1958, Chapters 1
and 2; Rank's 1903 autobiography is excerpted in Chapter 1),
Jones (1955-57, II and III), and Nin (1966-67). Page references
will be given only for points of special interest.

there was little encouragement for Rank to pursue his studies. When he was thirteen, his uncle directed him to take a workshop course as preparation for technical school. In 1933, the diarist Anaïs Nin recorded a conversation with Rank in which he said that "At an early age he was put to work in a glass blower's factory because his mother was a widow" (Nin, 1966-67, I, p. 278). No other source mentions his father's death or its exact date; at the very least, it can be assumed that Rank's father died before Rank met Freud.

Rank's own account of his early years is both ironic and cryptic. It is clear that he was miserable, lonely, in a state of turmoil, and given to thoughts of suicide. He read widely, including the works of Stendhal, Dostoevsky, Wedekind, Ibsen, and above all Nietzsche and Schopenhauer. He wrote poetry, fragments of several novels, and an analysis of each of Wagner's operas in terms of plot, characterization, development, and symbolic meaning (Taft, pp. 39-40). During the time that he was at technical school, his brother introduced him to the theater, and thereafter he attended it regularly.

From his diaries, it is clear that Rank had been reading Freud's available works by the year 1904. During 1905, he worked out the basic form of his psychoanalytic study of the artist, which, after later discussion with Freud and further revision, was published as *Der Künstler* (Rank, 1907). In 1906, he was bothered with lung trouble. By a later account, "A friend took him to Dr. Alfred Adler. During his physical examination they talked, and . . . Rank expounded some of his opinions of Dr. Freud's work. . . . Adler was so impressed with Rank that he introduced him to Freud" (Nin, I, pp. 278-79). From Freud's own account (1914a, p. 25), Rank first appeared with the completed draft of *Der Künstler* in

5

hand. From this impressive beginning, Rank quickly rose to a position of respect, admiration, and great usefulness within the psychoanalytic circle. In 1906 he became the secretary of the Psychological Wednesday Evenings (which became the Vienna Psychoanalytic Society in 1908), a position that he held until 1924. From 1906 on, he presented papers and vigorously participated in the scientific meetings of the society (see Nunberg and Federn, 1962). In 1908 he presented a brief note about Schiller's correspondence, which observation found its way into Freud's revision of *The Interpretation of Dreams* the next year (Jones, II, pp. 46-47; the note is recorded in Freud, 1909, pp. 102-03).

Freud was clearly drawn to Rank. He urged him to finish his education in the *Gymnasium* and the university, probably supported him financially both in his education and in his vacation travels (Jones, II, p. 104), and at the same time dissuaded him from becoming qualified as a doctor. (Rank and Sachs were the only nonmedical members of the pre-World War I circle.) Rank, for his part, took on major responsibilities and duties for Freud. He helped to found two psychoanalytic journals, as well as the psychoanalytic publishing company (*Internationaler Psychoanalytischer Verlag*). Until 1924 he served as the principal editor of the journals and the press. He carried out a variety of tasks for Freud himself: recataloging his library (in 1914; see Jones, II, p. 195); correcting proofs and updating bibliographic material for later editions of *The Interpretation of Dreams* (see Freud's prefaces to the third and fourth editions); and helping to trace mythological material for other writings (Jones, II, p. 405). According to Jones, Rank once joked that "Freud distributed references to other analysts' writings on the same principle as the Emperor distributed decorations, according to the mood and fancy of the moment" (*Ibid.*, p. 458). When Jones suggested the founding of a committee of six persons to regulate and safeguard the interests of psychoanalysis, Rank was an obvious choice as the person who had known Freud the longest.

Freud and Rank were also close personally. Hanns Sachs recorded that Rank was a regular weekly dinner guest at Freud's home (1944, p. 82), and that Rank regularly accompanied Freud on the walk home from meetings of the psychoanalytic society (*Ibid.*, p. 62), as well as that only Rank could keep up with Freud on long country walks (*Ibid.*, p. 109). In 1914, Rank took a holiday with Freud and also accompanied him to Budapest to attend the funeral of a former patient (Jones, II, p. 119).

Summing up the period before and immediately after World War I, Jones wrote:

> Rank would have made an ideal private secretary, and indeed he functioned in this way to Freud in many respects. He was always willing, never complained of any burden put upon him, was a man of all work for turning himself to any task, and he was extraordinarily resourceful. He was highly intelligent and quick-witted. (II, p. 181)

Rank's intellectual powers and analytic gifts were manifest in his publications of the prewar period. In addition to *Der Künstler*, there were *Der Mythus von der Geburt des Heldens* (The myth of the birth of the hero), in 1909; *Das Inzest-Motiv in Dichtung und Sage* (The incest motif in literature and legend) in 1912; and, in collaboration with Sachs, *Die Bedeutung der Psychoanalyse für die Geisteswissenschaften* (The significance of psycho-

7

analysis for the humanities) in 1913. Besides these major works, Rank also wrote numerous papers analyzing particular myths and legends (collected in Rank, 1919), as well as papers on psychoanalytic theory. Finally, he completed his doctorate (in German literature) in 1912 with a thesis titled *Die Lohengrinsage* (The Lohengrin legend).[2]

All of this changed soon after the war. Jones wrote that Rank "presented two quite different personalities before and after the first world war; I never knew anyone change so much. His personal experiences during the war brought out a vigour and other manifestations of his personality we had never suspected" (II, p. 180). To understand this change, it would be important to know about Rank's war experiences in detail; unfortunately, the available information is scanty and secondhand, apart from whatever unpublished correspondence may still exist. First, Rank had apparently arranged to visit Jones in London for a personal analysis in August 1914, but the outbreak of war made this impossible.[3] Freud wrote to Ferenczi in December 1914 that Rank was trying to avoid conscription, "fighting like a lion against his Fatherland" (Jones, II, p. 198). However, he was called up in June 1915, and the following January was transferred to Cracow (in Galicia, that part of Austria-Hungary that became part of Poland in 1919). He was the editor of the

---

[2] Curiously enough, in a 1930 summary and analysis of his writings, written well after the break with Freud, Rank still referred to this thesis as "probably the first one on psychoanalysis" at the University of Vienna.

[3] Jones (II, pp. 119, 181). Jones notes that apart from himself and Ferenczi, it was not the custom at this time for psychoanalysts to be themselves analyzed (II, pp. 182-83).

Krakauer Zeitung, the only German-language daily newspaper in Galicia and moreover the official journal of the armed forces for the region.[4] After 1915 he was separated from Freud and Vienna, except for a few brief visits and a few days' meeting with Freud in the resort town of Tatra (in Slovakia) in the summer of 1917. Jones noted, though without any evidence or description of detail, that Rank suffered two severe attacks of depression during this period, the later attack occurring toward the end of 1917 (II, p. 217). Finally, Rank met Beata Tola Mincer—"the woman who is created for me" (quoted in Taft, p. 70)—whom he married on November 7, 1918, shortly before the Armistice and his return to Vienna.[5] Rank was the first of the Vienna psychoanalytic circle to return after the war.

He quickly and energetically resumed his prewar duties. He was instrumental in founding the Verlag, which put the publication interests of the psychoanalytic movement on a secure basis. Until 1924 he was its general editor. He published a collection of his previous writings on myth and legend, as well as some further original work of this kind done during the war. He himself began to practice analysis for the first time after the war. Probably his own skill and his financial need were factors in this change; but Freud also needed someone who could take the patients that he himself could not, or did not wish to, analyze. Among this group were several

---

[4] In contrast, most of the other (medical) psychoanalysts were involved in medical work, often involving combat-related neuropsychiatric cases.

[5] Beata Rank became a child analyst and contributed numerous papers to the psychoanalytic journals (e.g., B. Rank, 1924).

9

Americans, some of whom invited him to New York in 1924 and subsequently formed the nucleus of a gathering that supported Rank's later ideas.

From this point several different problems slowly emerged. While it is beyond the scope of this introduction to evaluate the significance of all the relevant factors, it is appropriate to mention these problems because they occurred during the time that Rank wrote the first two versions of *The Don Juan Legend*. Chronologically, they are: (1) The conflict with Jones concerning the business affairs of the Verlag and the relationship between its Vienna and London branches (from about 1920); (2) Rank's book with Ferenczi, *Entwicklungsziele der Psychoanalyse* (Developmental goals of psychoanalysis), which proposed departures in technique and which disturbed Freud (Freud saw the manuscript in 1922; the book was published in 1924); (3) Freud's first operation for cancer of the palate (April 1923), with the resulting concern for his health and anxiety about his death; and (4) Rank's unexpected publication of *Das Trauma der Geburt* (The trauma of birth) in December 1923, which caused considerable debate, acrimony, and bitterness.

The conflict with Jones grew out of the complex relationship between the London and Vienna branches of the Verlag. The prospect of the vast English-speaking market for psychoanalytic writings convinced Freud that the London branch would, in the end, sustain not only the Vienna branch but the publications of psychoanalysis in general. At the same time, the drastic fall in the value of the Austrian currency indicated to both Jones and Rank that the most profitable course would be to print in Vienna and then ship books to London for sale, but this procedure would entail long delays in the transmittal of proofs in the race against time and the collapse of the Austrian currency. "Rank struggled heroically with the endless problems [of postwar Austria] and accomplished superhuman feats in coping with them almost single-handed," Jones wrote, while he himself had "a rather obsessive insistence on doing things in what I conceived to be the best way, with an impatience of sloppiness and a risk of provoking the sensibilities of other people concerned" (III, p. 48). The particular grounds of disagreement and misunderstanding multiplied; Rank displayed "an overbearing and hectoring tone. . . . over-ruling or ignoring. . . ." (*Ibid.*). The branches split apart in 1923.

The book with Ferenczi (Ferenczi and Rank, 1924) represented a slight change of emphasis in therapy: it was suggested that analysts should actively become involved in the transference of the patient, with a corresponding de-emphasis on interpretational penetration of analysis to the historic sources of the neurosis. Freud had read the manuscript and had made several suggestions; yet when the book did appear, he expressed some doubts. Other analysts, notably Jones, Abraham, and Rado, were even more disturbed. Rank himself dated his separation from the psychoanalytic movement from the publication of this book.[6]

Rank had heard directly from Freud's doctors about the malignancy that was discovered in the course of the first operation in the spring of 1923, before Freud himself

[6] "This [book] was my first parting, not from Freud, but from his whole ideology, which is erected on the fundamental importance of intellectual understanding as a curative factor." From Rank's remarks to the First International Congress on Mental Hygiene, Washington, D.C., May 8, 1930; quoted in Taft (p. 150).

or anyone else knew. According to Jones, Freud maintained that the news "had a fateful effect on Rank, who was entirely dependent on him for a living, and that it had stimulated Rank to strike out on an independent path" (III, pp. 57-58). There is, however, no independent evidence of Rank's reactions.

The principal problem, that most often identified as the real break between Rank and Freud, was of course the publication of *The Trauma of Birth* in December 1923 (the publication date is 1924). First of all, the appearance of the book was a complete surprise to everyone in the Vienna group. Sachs, who counted himself a close friend of Rank, recounts his dismay:

> He did not say a word about his new ideas to me until he presented me with a printed copy, although we had stayed at the same summer-resort and had seen each other daily while he was writing the book. (1944, pp. 60-61)

The actual content of the book precipitated a storm of confusion, dismay, and hostility. Because the themes of this book are relevant to some of Rank's interpretations of the Don Juan legend in the present book, they may be summarized briefly as follows: (1) The analytic situation is regularly symbolized by patients as birth, and in fact has numerous similarities to it (e.g., the couch as a symbol of the maternity bed). The ending of an analysis is a reproduction of the first separation from the mother, while resistance to ending analysis and transference express both a fixation on the mother and a hostility toward the father, who was responsible for the first separation from her. (2) Infantile anxiety, the prototype of all later anxiety, derives from fear of separation from the mother; only later is it displaced on to the father, because he prevents the return to the mother. (3) Sexuality is an attempt to overcome the trauma of birth by returning to the mother. The anxiety and ambivalence associated with birth (hence with the mother and, by association, with women in general) are reflected in a variety of perversions, as well as in both overestimation and underestimation of women. Women resolve this anxiety vicariously through reproduction; men cannot resolve it through a direct approach to the mother, because of the attendant anxiety that would thereby be aroused. This conflict is the real meaning of the Oedipus complex: men are driven to renounce the mother, and this renunciation recapitulates the primary (anaclitic) separation. (4) Psychoneuroses are regressions to the infantile wish to go back *completely* into the mother. (5) In terms of cultural prehistory, the renunciation of the mother postulated by Freud in *Totem and Taboo* actually occurs because although all of the men take sexual possession of the mother, not all of them can return into her. The "heroic lie" distorts this wish, so that only one son, the youngest, actually does so. (6) Society has gradually evolved into a patriarchy, with greater and greater exclusion of women, because of the painful memory of the birth trauma. The fear of the father which is so stressed in psychoanalytic theories of culture is in fact a displacement from the original fear of the mother. (7) The ambivalent attitude toward the mother is reflected in the development of technology, literature, religion, art, philosophy, and psychoanalytic knowledge itself.

Reaction to the book was strong. In Berlin, Abraham was hostile, while Sachs in Vienna thought the theory incomplete. Freud had discussed the theoretical ideas behind it with Rank over a year before. At the appearance of the book, Freud wrote to Ferenczi that "I don't know

13

whether 66 or 33 percent of it is true, but in any case it is the most important progress since the discovery of psycho-analysis" (March 1924; quoted in Jones, III, p. 61). He was alarmed that the theory might dissolve his own work, but he counseled patience and investigation of the value of the theories, both to Abraham in Berlin and to the committee generally. Finally, Freud was distressed at what he perceived to be the increasing incoherence and lack of order in Rank's style.

Events moved rapidly from this point. Rank announced that the committee was dissolved in a letter circulated ten days before the International Psychoanalytic Congress at Salzburg in April 1924. He left the conference itself after the second day to travel to America, a visit that had been previously arranged on invitation from the president of the New York Psychoanalytic Society (Jones, III, p. 71). Rank spent six months in New York lecturing and analyzing patients. His initial enthusiasm waned by the summer (Taft, pp. 96-97), and he returned to Vienna in the autumn. The Freud-Rank correspondence during his absence had ranged from assurances of loyalty to clear and blunt statements of differences on both sides. After inconclusive talks with Freud, Rank made his second departure from Vienna in November. At this same time, Freud received disturbing news from Brill about statements and claims Rank had made in New York and the departures from psychoanalysis that seemingly had been evoked in Rank's American pupils (Jones, III, p. 74). Rank travelled to Paris and after a severe attack of depression (according to Jones), returned to Vienna in December. After intense conversation with Freud, he was overwhelmed, "confessed" the neurotic basis of his theories, and attempted to undo their effect by apologetically asking forgiveness from the committee (*Ibid.*, pp. 76-77). From a very different point of view, Taft concludes a description of these events with the statement that "Anyone who has known Rank intimately could not doubt that he paid dearly for his freedom, in fear, conflict, illness, and suffering" (p. 109).

Rank travelled to America for the second time in January 1925; but he came back to Vienna at the end of February in a depressed state. Freud and Rank resumed fruitful intellectual discussion, with overtones of personal analysis; but Jones and Ferenczi continued to suggest that his ideas were obscure and unintelligible.[7] Rank then left for his third visit to America, returning to Vienna before the end of 1925. In April of 1926 he left for Paris: this time it was the final departure from Vienna and the definitive break with psychoanalysis.

The events of 1922-26 in Rank's life have been discussed in some detail because they are important to a full understanding of the situation in which he wrote *The Don Juan Legend* and later revised it. A careful study of the several versions of this book, together with further research on the correspondence between Rank and the other committee members would, I believe, be most valuable to a biographer's understanding of Rank himself and the reasons for his break with Freud.

The rest of Rank's life is beyond the purview of this

---

[7] Undoubtedly the death of his older brother Paul after the war also had an effect on Rank. Paul had been involved in managing the Vienna Association and the journals. Unfortunately, there is some uncertainty about the date of Paul's death. Jones said that it was in early 1925 (III, p. 77), while Taft gives January 1921 as the date (p. 73).

The criticism of Jones and Ferenczi referred to a paper Rank presented at the 1925 Psychoanalytic Congress, published as Rank (1926). Jones, III, p. 79; but see Taft, p. 117 for a contradictory evaluation.

introduction, and will be discussed only briefly. He developed new techniques of therapy and a new theory of personality (see Karpf, 1953; Munroe, 1955; Progoff, 1956, Chapter 7; Maddi, 1972, pp. 55-60, 304-07); he reworked his earlier writings on art and the evolution of culture into *Art and Artist* (1932a) and *Seelenglaube und Psychologie* (Psychology and the soul, 1930). He continued yearly visits to America, where he finally settled in 1934. During his time in the United States, he was involved in giving lectures and seminars at schools of social work in New York and Philadelphia, and he practiced therapy. His later ideas had some influence on Carl Rogers, some of the existential psychologists, and some neo-Gestalt therapists (J. Jones, 1968). His emphasis on therapy as a relationship, in contrast to Freud's emphasis on exploration and analysis, has infiltrated American psychoanalytic thinking (Waelder, 1960, pp. 79-80). In his last years, Rank was troubled by a variety of physical ailments (Taft, pp. 199-276 *passim*). He was divorced from his wife in June 1939 and remarried shortly thereafter. After a brief illness, he died rather suddenly and unexpectedly in New York on October 31, 1939.

RANK'S INTERPRETATION OF THE DON JUAN LEGEND

Rank apparently had been interested in the legend of Don Juan from an early age. On January 19, 1904, at the age of nineteen, he recorded in his plans for writing a drama about "Don Juan, the man who seeks for his ideal of woman and cannot find her" (diary entry quoted in Taft, p. 21). Preserved in the Rank papers is a letter from the publisher of Heckel's *Das Don Juan-Problem in der neueren Dichtung* (The Don Juan problem in modern poetry) which apparently accompanied a review copy of the book. This book was the first German language critical investigation of the Don Juan theme, and was published in 1915. The publisher's letter was sent on May 16, 1916, and refers to the editor's (Rank's) request dated May 12, 1916. Apparently Rank requested this book for review during his tenure as editor of the *Krakauer Zeitung*. On the back of the letter, Rank had noted page references from the Heckel book under the headings of *Gastmahl* (banquet), *Vater* (father), *Leporello*, and the names of various authors of German versions of Don Juan. While not conclusive, this evidence strongly suggests that Rank began to work on his analysis of the legend during World War I, while he was away from Vienna.

As Rank mentions in the opening sentences of the book, he was stimulated to write the first version of his interpretation by seeing an "outstanding" performance of Mozart's *Don Giovanni* at the Vienna Opera on November 21, 1921. (The program from this performance is preserved in the Rank papers.) Within five months, he had completed an analysis for presentation to the Psychoanalytic Association meeting and for publication.[8] The folder of his papers that is concerned with this study gives some suggestion of his energy and resourcefulness: notations penciled on the back of Verlag notepaper and cigar-box covers, annotated newspaper clippings, galley proofs of the *Imago* article with quotations from Rostand's play (which he acquired on April 4, 1922) appended.

The Don Juan Legend is in many respects a tour de

---

[8] The galley proofs for version *B* were sent to Rank in late May 1922.

force of Rank's early work: erudition and familiarity
with classical authors, myth, legend, and contemporary
accounts of varied cultural practices; restless energy that
sometimes distorts a clear line of argument in its enthusiasm; and a complete commitment to psychoanalytic
modes of explanation (in the versions written before the
break with Freud; the later versions show a complete renunciation of psychoanalysis). It is curious that Rank's
work is the only worthwhile extended psychological interpretation of the Don Juan legend[9]—a legend that in
terms of the number of versions is surely the most influ-
ential one in western literature, and one that, in its direct
treatment of the themes of sexuality fused with punishment and damnation, symbolizes western culture since
the era of imperial expansion around the year 1600.

Most interpretations of Don Juan take one of two
general lines of analysis: either Don Juan is driven by
some cosmic force, such as a longing for the ideal or the
infinite (E.T.A. Hoffman, 1814), or the pure essence of
sensuality (Kierkegaard, 1843); or else he is the apothe-
osis of the bored narcissist who is incapable of forming
ties to others (Stendhal, 1822), or who is utterly indif-
ferent to the consequences of his actions (Maeztu, 1938).
Jung (1938) suggests that Don Juan is the result of the
"mother complex," without being very lucid about why
and how.

[9] Other psychological studies of the Don Juan theme include
Marañón (1940), Worthington (1962), Pratt (1960), and Winter (1973, Chapter 6). Weinstein (1959) mentions some minor
interpretations. Reik (1945) and Fenichel (1945), among the
psychoanalysts, refer in passing to Don Juan. Curiously, I have
not been able to find any reference to the legend in any of
Freud's works, although Freud was very fond of Mozart's *Don
Giovanni* (Schur, 1972, p. 103).

18

Eighteen years after writing the first version of *The Don Juan Legend*, Rank had occasion to compile an analysis of all of his writings. (This analysis is preserved in the Rank papers.) He recorded that this work was influenced by Freud's *Group Psychology and the Analysis of the Ego* (Freud, 1921), especially Postscript B of that book, which describes the developmental sequence from the primal horde through fatherless matriarchy up to the emergence of individual psychology.[10] Rank summarizes the Don Juan work as follows:

> This with much of the material in the *Beiträge*[11] (1911- 1914) (written during the excitement of the war and hence not so well done) represents the Rankian view of discussions associated with Freud's *Group Psychology* (see Postscript B).

Rank's statement is tantalizingly imprecise about the exact meaning of "the excitement of the war;" moreover, most of the *Beiträge* essays were written *before* the war, and the Don Juan work was written three years *after* the war. Nevertheless, several events that did excite Rank occurred immediately before or else during the time he wrote *The Don Juan Legend*: his marriage, the pregnancy of his wife and the birth of his daughter, the conflicts with Jones, and his first efforts at clinical psychoanalysis, as well as the germination of the ideas in his book with Ferenczi and *The Trauma of Birth*.

[10] Freud, for his part, noted at the beginning of Postscript B that "What follows at this point was written under the influence of an exchange of ideas with Otto Rank," adding a specific footnote to Rank's *Imago* paper (version *B*) in the 1923 second edition (Freud, 1921, p. 135).

[11] *Psychoanalytische Beiträge zur Mythenforschung; gesammelte Studien aus den Jahren 1912 bis 1914* (Rank, 1919).

19

The interpretation of the Don Juan legend advanced by Rank in this book may be briefly summarized. After a brief introductory chapter in which he outlines an "Oedipal" interpretation of Don Juan—that the many seduced women represent the one unattainable mother, and that the many men whom he deceives, fights, and kills represent the father—Rank devotes three chapters to a discussion of the relationship between Don Juan and Leporello, his obedient but nevertheless critical servant. Leporello is proud of his master; yet he is a "cowardly, anxious, cringing soul." Rank quotes the servant's first words, which open the opera:[12]

> I want to be a gentleman,
> and I don't want to serve any more.
>
> . . . .
>
> Toiling by day and night. . . sleeping badly. . . .
>
> . . . .
>
> Don't count on me, master!
>
> . . . .
>
> If I could only get away from here. . . .

Rank notes that "the tragedy of Leporello is that always he is permitted to represent his master only in the painful and critical situations"; and he quotes (with his own emphasis) Heckel's discussion of Leporello as the "negative hero" who "cannot extricate himself," an "entirely innocent scapegoat" for his master's tricks. Rank then argues that the servant is in fact identical with the master, but is split off from him as his ego ideal—just as the avenging statue is split off as a later and more powerful representative of the ego ideal. These chapters are cast in terms of Rank's interpretation of the motif of the

[12] Quotations are translated from the German version of Da Ponte's libretto; see note 5 of Chapter 2.

double (see Rank, 1914), as well as earlier psychoanalytic discussion of how one personality is split into two or more different characters in a play.[13] Perhaps this extended discussion of the master-servant relationship reflected some of Rank's concern about his own relationship with Freud.

Chapter 4 discusses the origin of the ego ideal in the primary narcissism that is renounced, for reasons of fear, in favor of identification with the father. Such a process actually preserves the primary narcissism in a vicarious way, since the object of cathexis has been incorporated into the ego itself. In like manner, the distortions of the deed of slaying the primal father that were made by the first poet (and, in a more general sense, by the artist) make clear that in glorifying the hero he is really glorifying himself. Then follow two chapters on the statue—the father whom Don Juan has slain, and who returns to avenge his death by summoning Don Juan to the grave and judgment. Rank traces a line of presumed cultural evolution,[14] in which the belief that death is caused by the hostile wishes of a living person leads to guilt about these hostile wishes due to the fear that the dead will return to avenge their "murder." This guilty fear is the origin of numerous funeral practices, such as devouring, burning, or burying: practices designed to prevent

[13] The psychological significance of this dramatic device is further discussed in Fairbairn (1952, pp. 8-9).

[14] Chapters 5 and 6 are closely related to Freud's *Totem and Taboo* (1913), and, like that earlier work, uses the conceptions of nineteenth-century evolutionary anthropology, in which "primitive" cultures are thought to preserve vestiges of earlier periods of belief and social organization which "modern" cultures passed through in prehistoric times. Nevertheless, Kroeber's sympathetic reinterpretation of Freud's anthropology (Kroeber, 1939) can also be applied to Rank.

21

such a return. The motif of devouring is especially prominent in these funeral practices, and this motif is preserved in the characteristic manner of Don Juan's end—Don Juan and the statue invite each other to a banquet, at which the hero himself is finally "devoured" by the grave.[15]

Rank then turns to a discussion of the role of women in the legend in the last part of Chapter 6 and all of Chapters 7 through 9. He argues that the hostility of women toward Don Juan in the earliest versions of the legend is derived from the primal struggle to subdue the mother, who emerged as dominant after the slaying of the primal father. She protected the hero in order to use him as the instrument of her liberation; yet on the other hand, she feels animosity toward him because he is an inadequate replacement for the slain father.[16] Hence while superficially Don Juan struggles with the father, more profoundly he has foundered on the "mother complex"—a desire for the unattainable mother, rooted in the biological wish for exclusive possession of her. In the end, Don Juan fulfills this primal desire by being "swallowed" by the grave, which according to Rank is an obvious womb symbol. Rank then traces the emergence of the woman as Don Juan's principal antagonist in Mozart's *Don Giovanni* and in later versions, including that of Shaw and especially that of Rostand, which appeared

[15] Austen (1939) also discussed the similarity between various aspects of the Don Juan legend (particularly the end of the hero) and a variety of cultural practices; while his work is not as wide-ranging as Rank's, it does give more attention to the specifically Spanish beliefs and practices which presumably were part of the cultural heritage of the author of the first Don Juan play in Spain at the beginning of the seventeenth century.

[16] In this connection, see Rank's analysis of the legend of the faithless widow (Rank, 1913).

22

as Rank was writing the first manuscript of *The Don Juan Legend*. Rostand's work is, according to Rank, the culmination of the devaluation and characterological destruction of Don Juan: the avenging women gather and "reveal to him how pitiable his imagined seduction technique had been: the women conquered him; and if he left them, it was because the unadmitted fear of having to remain with one of them drove him to it."

I think that Rank's emphasis upon the role of women in the Don Juan legend is correct. More broadly, his stress on the child's relation to the mother as antecedent to and in some respects determinative of the later "Oedipal" relationship to the father seems in many respects to be a valid and useful supplement to "patrifocal" psychoanalytic theory, although few people would accept the specific terms of this relation as described in *The Trauma of Birth*. Within recent years, the mother-child relation has been a major focus of interest and theory in some schools of psychoanalysis, notably Klein (see Klein and Riviere, 1937), the "attachment" theorists (Bowlby, 1969), and the "object relations" school in general (e.g., Fairbairn, 1952; Balint, 1963). Whether Rank actually influenced these later theorists is not fully clear; Guntrip acknowledged the analogy between the birth trauma and traumatic object relations, but was not favorable toward Rank's theory (1961, p. 320).

The last chapter of this book deals with the psychology of the artist—one of a series of such studies that began with Rank's first book (Rank, 1907) and ended with his post-Freudian *Art and Artist* (Rank, 1932a). In the present book, Rank argued that the artist deals with the major complexes of mankind in such a way as to allay the anxiety that is associated with them. This means that the nature of the artistic product will vary from time to

23

time, according to which complexes are salient. In addition, there is a general process of development or evolution in the artistic treatment of any particular theme (i.e., complex). First is the "heroic" stage in which the original subject matter is so revised as to make unrecognizable the anxiety, or the motive stemming from the relevant complex. With time, successive elucidations of the subject matter make these original motives clear—as Mozart's opera and the later "psychological" versions of Don Juan did in the case of the true role of the woman. The original anxiety is, thereby, reactivated, so that the elucidation requires a devaluation of the subject in order to allay the anxiety. Thus the later Don Juan versions portray the hero as aged and feeble, or give a romantic explanation of the hero's character (e.g., his search for the mother becomes the "quest for the ideal woman").

The artist himself is driven by a strong primary narcissism to create his art as a replacement for the previous ego ideal of the masses (i.e., conscience, standards). Yet the satisfaction deriving from such an accomplishment is doomed to failure for two reasons. First, if the artist's work becomes popular, then it also thereby becomes the ego ideal of the masses, so that the artist has done nothing new. Second, his replacement of the ego ideal is actually a repetition of the primal act of slaying the father (i.e., the received ego ideal) in a psychological sense. At this point, the artist is driven to devalue his own prior work, or his previous ego ideal formations. According to Rank, such a process can always be detected both in the evolution of art itself, and in the work of any individual artist or poet *when that work falls into distinct periods*: the latter period is always a devaluation of the former one.

24

CHANGES IN RANK'S INTERPRETATION OF DON JUAN

In successive versions of *The Don Juan Figure*, Rank made the greatest changes from version C (1924) to versions F and G (1932 and after); but a careful reading of the manuscript, corrected proofs, and final version of B and C is also of interest.

At the beginning of the manuscript of B, Rank wrote that "after some hesitation I have decided to write down some observations . . ." on seeing the Mozart opera. In correcting the proofs (June 1922) he removed the reference to "hesitation" and switched the "I" to "we." In the second paragraph, a complex and tortured sentence that was several times revised in the actual manuscript shows evidence of uncertainty and ambivalence:[17]

> If one is disposed to approach the Mozart opera with a psychoanalytic point of view—a disposition which happened to suggest itself to the author through work with certain circles of thought. . . .

Rank seems to mean simply that inasmuch as he is a psychoanalyst, he will write a psychoanalytic interpretation; but what finally emerged displays both some uncertainty and a curiously passive mood. In the manuscript of B, after considerable rewriting about Freud, Rank noted that the transformation of faithfulness to the one mother into manifest treachery toward women, as in Don Juan, involves the operation of several defense mechanisms that are activated by guilt. In the proofs of

[17] "Ist man gerade in der Stimmung—wie sie zufällig dem Verfasser durch die Beschäftigung mit gewissen Gedankenkreisen nahe lag—. . . ." Rank's status as a nonmedical analyst, new to actual clinical practice, was at that time rather unclear.

B, however, he added the portentious advice that "when psychoanalysis is applied to an extra-analytic theme it can only serve as the starting point for advancing our understanding, rather than as a result that is known in advance and only has to be confirmed."[18] Rank apparently introduced this sentence between April and June 1922, during the time that his clinical paper on "potency" (Rank, 1923) was probably being discussed with Freud and others (see Taft, pp. 75-76).

Finally, Rank deleted from the proofs of *B* a final sentence in the penultimate paragraph of Chapter 1, a sentence advocating the "patient concentration" on analyzing defenses in order to "make understandable . . . the resistance of such intensive affect arising from a sense of guilt." This sentence was removed in 1922 during the time he was writing the first version of the monograph on technique (Ferenczi and Rank, 1924), and may reflect the themes of that monograph.

The book then turns to the master-servant relationship between Don Juan and Leporello. As noted in Chapter 4 of the translation (note 5), Rank originally included a reference to the "coarse jokes" of Don Juan's servant in the German puppet plays, in the context of a discussion of those versions in which Don Juan actually slays his own father. In the final version of *B*, this specific reference is removed to Chapter 9, in the general context of

---

[18] Compare the following passage in Ferenczi and Rank (1924, p. 32), which was written during the summer of 1922 and later revised: "The connected recounting of complexes, or the attributes of these, may have its place in descriptive psychology, but not in the practical analysis of the neurotic, nor does it even belong in the psycho-analytic study of literary, or ethno-psychological products where it must undoubtedly lead to a monotony in no way justified by the many sidedness of the material. . . ."

the devaluation of the hero through the power of women, and the specific context of those versions which emphasize both the enfeeblement of Don Juan (the "master") and his nature as "a criminal absolutely unrestrained by any thoughts of conscience, who would fashion an *eating utensil* out of the *bones* of those who perished through his fault." Perhaps this change reflects, through displacement and rationalization, the evolution of Rank's feelings about Freud.

The final changes that Rank made in 1922 involve the role of women. In the manuscript of *B*, Rank noted that Don Juan is no darling of women in the original versions, but rather that he "does not shrink from disguise and false promises of marriage." In *B* itself, this is changed into "shrinks from no weapon and *therefore* he actually struggles against the women as he does against the men." During this period (April-June 1922) Rank thus focussed on the theme of men's ambivalence toward women as an element of a struggle that is primary, and not to be derived solely from a phallic preoccupation with serial seduction. The theme was to receive fuller treatment in *The Trauma of Birth*, but the changes made in the present book enable us to date this altered focus more precisely—in fact, at just the time of Freud's criticism of Rank's clinical papers and the book with Ferenczi. Rank further altered his views at this time about the reasons for the ascendancy of women to positions of power. Originally, he simply quoted Freud's interpretation that the women had power because of the mutual opposition of the brothers (Freud, 1913, p. 144, and 1921, p. 135). However, in the final version of *B*, he referred to this as "Freud's hypothesis."

Rank introduced greater changes in version *C*, which appeared about two years after *B* and subsequent to the

27

publication of *The Trauma of Birth*. In the second paragraph of the opening chapter, where he articulates his relationship to psychoanalysis, reference to "the psychoanalytic point of view" became reference to "a psychoanalytic point of view." At the same time, there is further elaboration of the master-servant relationship. Footnote 2 of Chapter 2 about Leporello's dissatisfaction at the beginning of the opera is now embellished with three actual quotations from the libretto, concluding with "If I could only get away from here. . . ." The hero justifies his behavior with Leporello's wife with the observation that "I have only got even for what you did to me."[19] In *B*, Rank called this a "secret motive," but in *C* he called it a "deep motive of revenge, and clearly illuminating the interchangeability of master and servant." In version *G*, Rank further described this passage as Don Juan's "abuse" of Leporello. The analytically oriented reader may discern in these subtle changes further evidence of Rank's attitude toward Freud.

The interpretation of the role of women along the lines of the birth trauma theory is further emphasized in *C*. After the discussion of women in early myths and the hypothetical reconstruction of woman's role in prehistory, Rank concluded Chapter 7 in version *B* with the following cautious words:

> But in this free reconstruction of the prehistorical fate of woman our fantasy has perhaps prevailed on too uncertain a foundation. Thus we turn to what the authoritative Don Juan poems have to say about the role of the woman.

[19] As noted in note 5 of Chapter 2, this analysis is based on a line that appears only in the German translation of Da Ponte's libretto and not in the Italian original, but the point is irrelevant for present purposes.

28

In C this is replaced by two paragraphs which confidently suggest that the real Don Juan fantasy of conquering countless women is to be traced back to the infantile tendency to regress to fusion with the mother, which can only be partly achieved because of her ultimate unattainability. Rank further held that the death of the hero is itself a fuller satisfaction of the primal tendency toward fusion with the mother—a marked departure from his previous interpretation whereby the hero's end was due to guilt feelings and a consequent tendency toward punishment—a tendency that arose from the ego ideal, and is personified in the father figure of the statue. (This earlier interpretation is also preserved in C.) "In the figure of the Stone Guest, who also represents the coffin, the mother herself appears, coming to fetch the son." Rank then added a new final paragraph introducing the study of the role of women in the Don Juan versions in order to show that the new interpretation "is not just in the service of a predetermined opinion or psychoanalytic theory." In introducing the early twentieth-century Don Juan versions of Friedmann, Bernhardi, and Rostand, in which the ghosts of Don Juan's female victims return to torment him, Rank changed his description of the motif from "perhaps sentimental" to "perhaps original, but in any case altered in a sentimental direction." The issue is the analytic stance toward the "feminization of conscience" and the appearance of the powerful woman. On the one hand, Rank argued that they are merely a displacement from the band of avenging brothers; yet on the other hand, his matrifocal theory of individual development and cultural evolution here conflicts with that orthodox interpretation (as well as with most of version C as a whole)—for now the powerful women are taken as the *original* meaning, the original situation, and the original motive of the legend.

Finally, Rank sharpened the contrast between artistic creation and the psychoanalytic process in the introduction to the final chapter on the social function of art and the nature of the artist. In the course of the evolution of the presentation of any particular theme, the original motive becomes elucidated, though in a devalued way. The articulation of this unconscious motive then reaches a limit. In *B*, Rank wrote that "beyond this limit is the domain of psychoanalysis, which through intellectual means is able to lead back to the original value [of the motive], and no longer devalues it on affective grounds." In *C*, the function of psychoanalysis is described in much more mixed terms: it "is able to judge and criticize on an intellectual basis rather than devaluing on affective grounds." Thus by 1924 Rank had begun to develop his later view that the work of psychoanalysis was by no means an unmixed blessing, especially to the creative artist (see Rank, 1930 and 1932a).

Version *F* contains much of the illustrative detail of the prior versions, but in a wholly different context of theory and interpretation. In fact, it is a completely different book. Since a complete discussion of this work would involve considerable elucidation of Rank's later views on personality and cultural evolution, I shall indicate only the main lines of departure from the earlier versions, using the manuscript *G* (presumably a draft for an English translation) as indicating Rank's final views on the Don Juan legend.

In version *G* Rank completely abandoned any attempt to explain Don Juan in terms of psychoanalytic concepts or mechanisms, including the quasi-analytic notions of birth trauma theory such as the "mother complex." In fact he argued that it was impossible to understand the Mozart opera purely from the standpoint of individual psychology: the legend represents a "revolutionary change which cannot be genetically traced from the individual complexes, but can only be made intelligible through the understanding of the historical development of folk-tradition."

Don Juan is now taken to represent the struggle between materialism and spiritual forces; in individual terms, between the ordinary self and the immortal soul. Don Juan is condemned because he doubts the grace of God—he "has only reckoned with earthly values, and not with the spiritual force whose vengeance overtakes him" in the statue of the Commander. These spiritual forces are derived from Christian transformations of universal themes: the eternal longing for immortality becomes, in Christian thought, the belief in the immortality of the spirit and thus the rejection or devaluation of the purely mortal and material world. Don Juan is thus identified with the Christian devil as the incarnation of concern with purely material, instinctual values. As such, he acts out of a fear of losing his mortal soul through marriage and children; hence he is antagonistic toward women. In fact he personifies the ancient rite of the *jus primae noctis*, by which powerful superior beings were thought to impregnate women in order to protect the soul of the husband from the jeopardy that would otherwise befall it through the process of reproduction. In Christian terms, this belief in the mortal self and the practices associated with it have become stigmatized as sexual libertarianism, so that Don Juan is punished and dies for his "violation of the Church's belief in the soul." Such a brief summary does not do full justice to this complex and rather confusing revision of an already complex book; but I hope that it makes clear how far Rank's final interpretation of the Don Juan legend departed from his earli-

31

er writings on the subject. Since the purpose of this translation is to bring before the English reader a psychoanalytic account of the most popular legend in western literature, I feel that the present brief account of versions *F* and *G* is sufficient. The reader who wishes to pursue Rank's later ideas in relation to the Don Juan legend is directed to his *Psychology and the Soul* (Rank, 1930).

Rank apparently omitted the entire last chapter from versions *F* and *G*. In one sense, they were irrelevant to these later works, for they involved a psychoanalytic outline of the personality of the artist and the function of art, in the tradition of his first publication (Rank, 1907). By 1932, Rank had come to repudiate the very worth of such an enterprise, for he felt that art and artist, as well as morale and culture itself, were threatened by the forces of rational materialism and analysis:

> This process of increasing extension of consciousness in humanity, which psycho-analysis has fostered so enormously in the last decades—but not entirely to the advantage of mankind as a whole—was prophesied by me in my *Künstler* in 1905 (at the time of my first acquaintance with Freud) as likely to be the beginning of a decay of art. . . . And although the Oedipus complex, and the sexual problem of the child that is bound up with it, still forms the centre [of the psychoanalytic interpretation of art], this is rather the sign of a fatal stoppage than a proof of the superlative importance of this family problem. (Rank, 1932a, pp. 375, 63; see also Rank, 1941)

In the final *G* version, Rank devalued his previous interpretation of Don Juan ("such an [psychoanalytic] interpretation . . . is inadequate when it treats of a popular literary motif"); he turned away from his previous work on art and artist; and he repudiated the connection with Freud and psychoanalytic theory.

Most striking is Rank's changed treatment of the effect of the father's death on the creations of the artist. He concluded the present book with the observation that Mozart's father died as Mozart began the music for *Don Giovanni*, and his best friend died during the course of the work. The death of the father should, Rank suggested, arouse "deeply ambivalent stirrings" of guilt, which are fused with unchecked sensuality "through the suppleness and immediacy of musical expression . . . the hero's conflict of conscience . . . and the passionate rhythm of an unbroken conquering nature." In version *G*, Rank deleted the discussion of the two emotions in conflict and fusion and withdrew all psychoanalytic interpretation of the father's death. Finally, he placed this passage at the very beginning of the book, in the context of an interpretation of the impetus for Mozart's frenzied creation of *Don Giovanni* as "solace for his oppressed soul," adding as an opening challenge that "it is impossible to comprehend this work of art purely from the standpoint of individual psychology."

A passing reference to the same episode in Mozart's life in *Art and Artist* suggests the final resolution, for Rank, of the problem of the artist as the primal hero, driven by conscience and guilt:

> [The egoistical artist-type] needs, as it were, for each work that he builds, a sacrifice which is buried alive to ensure a permanent existence to the structure. . . . The frequent occasions when a great work of art has been created in the reaction following upon the death of a close relation seem to me to realize those favorable cases

33

for this type of artist in which he can dispense with the killing of the building's victim because that victim has died a natural death and has subsequently, to all appearances, had a monument piously erected to him (Rank, 1932a, p. 49).

THE DON JUAN LEGEND

DON JUAN

The only hero whom mankind admires!
Why, read their books, observe their plays, and find
Abundant proof! Mark with what lustful eyes
Virtue detests me! What do pond'rous louts
Expect from power, save a little while to be
What I am always? Mark the zeal,
The envious zeal, with which professors nose
Into my life? Who does not secretly
Admire the kiss I dared and he dared not,
Because of cowardice or ugliness?
I make them homesick, all of them! There is
No deed—despite thy serpent's hiss—no faith,
No knowledge, and no virtue, save it springs
From grief at being other than myself!

THE DEVIL

What can you keep?

DON JUAN

What Alexander's dust
Has kept, the joy of knowing that it was
Almighty Alexander! Only, I
Am all my army, and 'tis I myself
That have possessed!

THE DEVIL

You have possessed? It is
A victor's word, but, dear immoralist,
Pray, what have you possessed?

DON JUAN

Ho, Sganarello!
(*Enter Sganarello.*)
My list!

Edmond Rostand,
La dernière nuit de Don Juan
(first part)*

---

* *The Last Night of Don Juan*. English translation
adapted from that of T. L. Riggs, published by Kahoe
and Company, Yellow Springs, Ohio, 1929.

1.

PSYCHOANALYTIC
INTERPRETATION OF THE
DON JUAN LEGEND

THE IMMORTAL name of the Spanish love hero,
with its magical sound, instinctively evokes a series of
erotic images and anticipations that appear indissolubly
bound up with it. We have decided to write down under
this title certain reflections and thoughts which were
stimulated by an outstanding performance of Mozart's
masterpiece [*Don Giovanni*] at the Vienna Opera (November 13, 1921). Yet it must be said in advance that we
shall discuss only a few of the generally fascinating aspects of the Don Juan figure. We shall say even less of
Mozart, who had perhaps an even greater share in the
immortality of his hero (as seems obvious to us from
the fact that this musical version of the material, which
is so popular with poets, remains the only one of enduring and profound effect).[1]

If one is straightaway disposed to approach the Mo-

---

[1] [Rank's judgment of Mozart's opera is shared by most literary
scholars (e.g. Mandel, 1963, p. 21). Certainly *Don Giovanni*
was the most popular and familiar version of the Don Juan legend during the nineteenth century. Yet Shaw and more recent
writers argue that the original Spanish play by Tirso de Molina
(see below, note 7) is an enduring and brilliant work in its own
right. Probably this play was not available in a good German
translation in Rank's time.]

zart opera from a psychoanalytic point of view—a dis-
position which happened to suggest itself to the author
through work with certain circles of thought—then to
some extent one excludes from consideration the conscious goals of the erotic hero. Thus one notes readily
(though not without surprise) that the action portrays
anything but a successful sexual adventurer; on the contrary, it presents a poor sinner pursued by misfortunes,
who finally arrives at the destiny of the Christian hell
that is appropriate to his era and background. Imagining
the happy, gratifying time of the real Don Juan is left
to the fantasy of the audience—who appear only too
happy to make use of this privilege[2]—while the stage is
given over to presentation of the tragic features of the
moral law. Therefore, in submitting this obviously painful aspect of Don Juan to psychoanalytic scrutiny, we
are merely following the path indicated by tradition and
poetry.

Thus our interest is first directed away from the finished form [of the legend] toward its development; yet
even a quick glance at the numerous incarnations of Don
Juan[3] shows us that we can find no clarification there.
For the type immortalized by Mozart enters into literature fully developed,[4] while the easy conqueror of wom-

[2] [The manuscript of *B* adds here: "—yes, and apparently
even to abuse it, while at the same time they will not let the
tragic hero enter into their thoughts," in place of the rest of the
sentence.]

[3] [In the manuscript of *B*, Rank first wrote and then crossed
out: "although (in number) they almost approach the love objects of the hero."]

[4] "The oldest Don Juan version in world literature is the
Spanish comedy that appeared before 1620 in two slightly

en, so familiar to popular consciousness through its traditions, has in fact never existed. Consequently we can conclude that the essence of the Don Juan material is more profound than the frivolous breaking of hearts; rather, that from the beginning the legend and drama must have sought and found something else. The typical erotic love hero, even in such a grand manner, probably could be represented more easily and perhaps better by another figure.[5] On the other hand, the Christian spectacle of hell, so laden with all the guilt feelings of original sin, also would seem to us as strange as the surviving medieval religious morality plays, if great men and artists had not rescued them in the way that Goethe created Faust out of the spiritual puppet play of the sorcerer, or in the manner in which Shakespeare created Hamlet out of the earlier ghost dramas. They have recovered the universal human content, stripping away all kinds of overgrown accretions and expressing it in eternal symbols.

The tradition clearly shows that the description of unbounded sexuality was not the principal motif of the Don Juan material. Nor do we need to consider the plain historical evidence that a real Don Juan figure never existed[6] in order to confirm our assumption that the un-

---

different versions: *El Burlador de Sevilla* and *¿Tan Largo Me Lo Fiáis?*" (Heckel, 1915).

[5] See Schmitz (1913).

[6] "The opinion that has been firmly held for centuries, that Don Juan Tenorio (chamberlain of the Castillian king Pedro the Cruel) was the model for the Burlador, is recognized as an error through the research of Farinelli [1896] and others. . . . It can be taken as certain that the author of the *Burlador* chose the name of a recognized personality for his hero, without there being any connection between this person and the events on the

checked, conquering nature of the hero is really a poetic fantasy construction; for this view is fully confirmed by the results of research in literary history. From the legendary traditions, the author of the *Burlador* took only the theme of the dead man, who was mocked, getting revenge on the arrogant blasphemer (i.e., the Burlador).[7]

> *It was left to the author of the* Burlador *to make the offender a seducer of women in the grand manner*; and to that extent he deserves the credit for making of his hero the first recognizable Don Juan. . . . The *Burlador* already laid the essential foundations; 150 years later would be erected on them the splendid structure in which the Don Juan material finds its most gifted formulation—Mozart's *Don Giovanni*. (Heckel, 1915, pp. 7-8 [Rank's emphasis])

Again in agreement with our view, we also see that the literary development of the Don Juan material prior to Mozart does not elaborate the seduction motif that is so attractive and poetic to the popular consciousness.

---

stage" (Heckel, 1915, p. 6). [See Wade (1969, pp. 27-40) for more recent evidence about this assertion, which is certainly disputable.]

[7] [The Spanish word "burlador" means literally "trickster," but with the strong connotation of "seducer" or "sadistic jokester" (see Wade, 1969, pp. 46-47). For studies of these earlier legends, see Austen (1939), MacKay (1943), Weinstein (1959), and Wade (1969). The conclusion of recent scholarship is that Tirso de Molina, generally acknowledged as the author of *El Burlador de Sevilla*, was the first to combine in a single character or theme the prior legends of (1) the easy seducer of a series of women, and (2) vengeance meted out by a dead man who had been mocked by the seducer.]

Rather, as though under a mysterious force, it elaborates the ancient, painful-tragic motif of guilt and punishment. In a superficial way this is already indicated by the double title of the first play by Tirso de Molina: *El Burlador de Sevilla y Convidado de Piedra* [The trickster of Seville and the stone guest], for the second part of the title—"The Stone Guest" [or "Stone Banquet"]—is the title of most Don Juan plays until the middle of the eighteenth century; while the imposing name of the hero does not appear at all in the title.[8] Thus by keeping to the tradition that the motif of guilt and punishment is more meaningful than that of sexuality, we have narrowed down the problem of investigation.

On the basis of psychoanalytic theory, we are prepared to derive such forces of overwhelming guilt and punishment—connected with strongly sexual fantasies—from the Oedipus complex. Clearly the endless series [of seduced women] along with the "injured third party"[9] characteristics of the Don Juan type appear to confirm this analytical interpretation: that the many women whom he must always replace anew represent to him the *one* irreplaceable mother; and that the rivals and adversaries whom he deceives, defrauds, struggles against, and finally even kills represent the *one* unconquerable mortal enemy, the father. This psychologically elemental fact has been discovered through the analysis of individuals; yet when psychoanalysis is applied to an extra-analytic theme it can only serve as the starting point for advancing our

[8] See the summary of poetic versions of the Don Juan material at the end of Heckel (1915) [and also the fuller and more recent lists by Weinstein (1959) and Singer (1965)].

[9] See Freud's fundamental essay, "A special type of choice of object made by men" (Freud, 1910b).

understanding, rather than as a result that is known in advance and only has to be confirmed.[10] For the transformation of this type, who in his unconscious remains true to the inviolable mother,[11] into the treacherous,

[10] It appears to me that Leo Kaplan's essay on the Don Juan legend (1921) is of this type. Only at the conclusion does it manifest an approach to one of the real problems.

[11] One version of the tradition about the model for the Don Juan figure, that of Don Miguel de Mañara (born 1626 in Seville), has developed this trait of faithfulness into pathology, so that the story almost seems to be the male counterpart of the legend of the faithless widow. [See Rank (1913b) on this legend and its psychoanalytic interpretation.] At the age of thirty, Mañara married Girolina Carillo de Mendoza. He loved his wife more than life itself, and when she died, he nearly lost his mind. Tormented by unrestrained grief, he fled with the body of his beloved to the mountains. After he had assuaged his sorrow somewhat, he finally sought consolation and peace in a monastery. However, when he came to Seville once again, the old wounds reappeared and made him the victim of tragic delusions. Often it seemed to him as though he were present at his own funeral. If he went out into the street, there suddenly appeared before his eyes a woman who, in an illusion, resembled the dead Girolina both in figure and manner. This woman would quickly withdraw from the encounter; if she turned around toward her pursuer, she would stare at him out of the empty eye sockets of a skull. In order to free himself from this terrible delusion, and to atone for the past sins of his worldly sensuality, Don Miguel devoted himself with glowing fervor to religious devotions and difficult penances. He made lavish donations to the church, and humbled himself to the role of a *servant* of the poor and the wretched—to being the person who washes corpses. Henceforth he spent his days among the corpses of convicted criminals, which he washed and anointed with loving hands. Later, when he approached death, he set down his last wishes in the following testament:

> I command and direct that immediately after my death, my body be stretched out on a cross of ashes, as the stat-

cynical person who despises women presumes the operation of repression, displacement, and transvaluation.[12] By tracing the paths and mechanisms of these processes, we have often learned our most important and interesting lessons.

After these limitations and justifications, we return to the Mozart opera as the point of departure. Two problems chiefly attract our attention: the first involves

---

utes of our order [of Calatrava] command; barefoot and wrapped in the shroud of my cloak, with a cross at the hood, two candles, and my head uncovered. In this way should my corpse be carried into the church of Santa Caridad: in a humble bier, led by twelve priests and no more, without pomp or music. It should be buried in the cemetery of this church, outside the gate, so that everyone steps and tramples on me. Thus shall my foul body, which is not worthy to rest in the Temple of God, be buried. And it is my will that a stone measuring two feet [three-quarters of a *vara*] square be placed on top of my grave, inscribed with these words:

HERE LIE THE BONES AND ASHES OF THE WORST MAN WHO EVER LIVED IN THE WORLD. PRAY TO GOD FOR HIM.

[Rank's footnote on Mañara was added in version C. It is perhaps based on an article, "Das Urbild des Don Juan—Neue Forschungen" in the *Neues Wiener Journal*, February 13, 1923. A fragment of the article is preserved in the Rank papers.

I have translated the testament from the original Spanish, as cited in Granero (1961, p. 604). Since Don Miguel de Mañara was born after Tirso de Molina wrote the *Burlador*, he clearly could not have been the model for Don Juan; nevertheless, scholars have often commented on similar elements in the two stories, and Mérimée (1834) explicitly mixed the Mañara and Don Juan legends. See Weinstein (1959, pp. 104-118) for a full discussion.]

[12] [The German *Umwertung* is used by Freud to indicate the process which Nietzsche described as the "transvaluation of values," and so I have translated it thus here.]

the topic of artistic form, and the second involves some analysis of content. Although these two problems differ basically in character, psychologically they are closely connected with each other and with the essence of the Don Juan material. In the end the problem of the material refers to the affect connected with guilt and punishment, and the problem of form involves the process of fantasy construction and the social function of art.

2.

DON JUAN AND LEPORELLO

Following our orientation, we direct our gaze away from the surpassing figure of Don Juan. Our attention is then drawn to a striking characteristic of his no less famous servant Leporello, a characteristic that, after a short digression, leads back again to the hero. On the one hand, this servant is really a friend and confidant in every love intrigue; yet on the other hand, he is certainly not a willing companion and helper, but rather a cowardly, anxious, cringing soul who is concerned only for his own interest. In his first aspect, he permits himself unbounded critical observations ("The life that you are leading is that of a good-for-nothing!"). He demands—and perhaps also gets—a share in kind of the prey of his master.[1] In his second aspect, he fearfully tries to avoid every danger. Very often he refuses further service[2] and is kept on only with money and threats. To complete the picture of the servant, he nibbles scraps from the banquet table even while he is serving.

One could say, "Like servant, like master," and thus

---

[1] [Leporello's direct participation in the conquests of his master is brought out by Mozart; in the *Burlador*, it is present but only in a vicarious form.]

[2] He is dissatisfied even the first time he sings: "Toiling day and night . . . sleeping badly"; the second time, "Don't count on me, master!"; a little later, "If I could only get away from here"; and so forth. [The second quotation is not in Da Ponte's original libretto; it is a modification introduced in the German translation by Rochlitz. See note 5 in this chapter. Version *B* has only the first nine words of this footnote.]

point out that Don Juan permits him these liberties because he needs him. For example, just before the famous
"catalogue" aria,[3] when Donna Elvira demands an explanation from the hero, he evades this painful situation
and pushes forward Leporello. Even before she is aware
of what is happening, the adroit adventurer has disap-
peared and *in his place* Leporello reads to her the list of
abandoned women, with the proper servant's pride that
comes from identification with the power [*Herrschaft*]
of the master.

This touches on a motif that is more clearly developed
in the course of the action, but one which is already
present as a motto in Leporello's first words at the beginning of the opera: "I want to be a gentleman, and I
don't want to serve any more." The tragedy of Leporello
is that he is permitted to represent his master only in the
painful and critical situations. Thus a second time, during
the vain attempt to seduce Zerlina, Don Juan would
punish his servant as the guilty one. In what seems to
Leporello to promise a delightful adventure, Don Juan
next exchanges cloak and hat with him in order to seduce Donna Elvira's chambermaid, while Leporello is
to take the abandoned lady for himself. Though amusing at the outset, this adventure only leads to his harm;
for in the meantime the steadily increasing band of those
bent on revenge (Donna Anna, Octavio, Masetto, Zerlina) have pursued Don Juan to Donna Elvira's house,

---

[3] [Act I, Scene 2: Leporello sings, "This is a catalogue of
beauties my master has loved. . . . In Italy, six hundred forty; in
Germany, two hundred thirty-one, . . . but in Spain there are
already a thousand and three," etc. Some productions of *Don
Giovanni* suggest that in this aria Leporello is not so much the
proud servant as he is, momentarily, the split-off conscience of
Donna Elvira.]

where they seize the presumed criminal, who finally turns out to be Leporello, protesting his innocence and begging for mercy.

The adroitness with which he frees himself from this dangerous situation, by suddenly disappearing, gives us a clue that he is more than a mere pupil of his master, that he is perhaps identical with him. But before we can explain what this might mean, we shall refer to the scene just before this one and the scene that follows it; both clearly confirm the identity of master and servant. They demonstrate not only that Leporello represents his master on occasions when a personal appearance would be painful, but that Don Juan plays the role of Leporello—as with Donna Elvira's chambermaid, and in a subsequent episode (which is only recounted) that leads on to the banquet, which is the second part of the Don Juan drama. As master and servant meet again in the cemetery after the episode of exchanging garments, something they were lucky to survive, Don Juan tells of another adventure that he has had in the meantime, an adventure which he owes to the switch of identity with his servant. Leporello at once supposes that the adventure could only have been with his wife, and reproaches his master for finding this so amusing.[4] Don Juan observes that "I have only got even for what you did to me"[5]—thus betraying a

[4] [Version *G* has "reproaches his master for this abuse."]

[5] [Rank's analysis is based on a German translation of *Don Giovanni* that departs in some respects from the original Italian libretto of Da Ponte. The translation of Friedrich Rochlitz (*Don Juan oder der Steinerne Gast*, Leipzig, Breitkopf u. Härtelschen Musikhandlung, 1801) was the source of most of the productions—actually adaptations—of the opera that were performed in Austria and Germany during the nineteenth century, and the version that Rank saw in Vienna in 1921 was almost certainly based on it. (A copy of the program for that

deep motive of revenge in his behavior, and clearly illuminating the interchangeability of master and servant. At this moment the voice from the statue of the Commander sounds ("Audacious one, let the dead rest in peace!"), and the second theme of the banquet of the dead begins—a theme that apparently is only loosely added on to the Don Juan material. We shall postpone discussion of it in order to ask ourselves what this identity of the two figures of Don Juan and Leporello means, and what it can contribute to the understanding of the plot, the development of the Don Juan figure, and the psychology of the poet and the audience.

---

performance, in the Rank papers, does not indicate the translation that was used, but the title, *Don Juan*, does suggest that it was a German-language version.) The Rochlitz translation has numerous alterations and additions, especially in the recitatives, which are relevant to Rank's analysis. The last part of the dialogue between Leporello and Don Juan, to which Rank refers here, is reproduced fully in the 1903 German version by Carl F. Wittman (Braunschweig: Henry Litolffs Verlag). I have italicized those words not in Da Ponte's libretto as reproduced in the version of Bleiler (1964):

> Leporello: Why not? How can you ask that! If it had been my wife?
> Don Juan: All the better! *I have only got even for what you did to me. One could die with laughter. Ha-ha-ha-ha!*
> Statue: Audacious one, let the dead rest in peace!

The Da Ponte libretto has the statue's first words as "Your laughter will cease before dawn!", with the other words occurring after Don Juan and Leporello express surprised curiosity; but the Wittman version simply uses the "Audacious one" remark twice.]

3.

LEPORELLO AS EGO IDEAL

WE must above all be clear that, in expressing such a formulation involving the identity of Don Juan and Leporello, we have already departed from the basis of the usual literary-aesthetic considerations in favor of a psychological interpretation that completely disregards the overt meaning of the figures. Thus, for example, in Heckel's description of the striking characteristic of Leporello we have not so much the portrait of a whole personality, but rather an intimation of the close psychological connection between these two figures (1915, p. 24):[1]

> As this *negative hero* is bound to the audacious seducer, who does not tremble before death and the devil; as he always wishes to be free from him and yet *cannot extricate himself* from the spell of the stronger personality;[2] as he time and again becomes the *scapegoat* for the tricks of his master, tricks of which he is *entirely innocent*; that has, in the deepest sense, an almost tragic effect.

We cannot imagine Don Juan without his servant and helper Leporello. This is not only a consequence of their actual dependence on each other as expressed in the plot, but is much more an intuitive sense of their psychological connection as a poetic effect. By this we mean that

[1] Emphases mine [Rank's].
[2] [In version *B*, a question mark in brackets—i.e., Rank's own insertion—was added here.]

the poet has neither taken this "negative hero" from real life, nor invented him for the purpose of enlivenment or contrast in the plot; rather, that the figure of Leporello is a necessary part of the artistic presentation of the hero himself. It would be an agreeable task to demonstrate the generality of this mechanism of poetic creation in a whole series of works, for in doing so one could show that the most elegant examples are to be found in the greatest writers of world literature. For our purposes it is sufficient that one such example has been pointed out in the psychoanalytic literature—and indeed, by Freud himself (1916, in connection with an observation by Jekels, 1917), who believed that Shakespeare often split up one character into two persons, each of which appeared incompletely comprehensible as long as one did not put the one together with the other into a unity. We find the same fashioning of mutually complementary characters in all great literary art; from its elementary expression in a Cervantes, Balzac, Goethe, or Dostoevski up through the modern "psychologizing" literature, which has sought to give a more or less conscious account of this artistic problem of form. We are not concerned with the notion that the poet projects a part of his own ego on to the figures of his fantasy—a notion which has already become psychologically banal, and which Léon Daudet, for example, has recently tried to substantiate again in his book *L'Hérédo: Essai sur le Drame Intérieur* (1916) by use of the heredity doctrines of the French psychiatrists.[3] Rather, we are here con-

[3] Occasionally a real poet also succeeds at this; for example, Alphonse Daudet, who has his most famous heroes conduct an excellent self-dialogue, between Tartarin-Quijote and Tartarin-Sancho. This psychic mechanism is also clear in Balzac's poetic figures, and Balzac was fully conscious of this. Even at the age

cerned with a very special, secondary division (as it were) of one form into two figures, who together constitute a complete, understandable, and unified character —as for example Tasso and Antonio in Goethe, or Shakespeare's Othello, who can be so naive and credulous because his jealousy is split off in the figure of Iago.

In a like manner, it would be impossible to create the Don Juan figure, the frivolous knight without conscience and without fear of death or the devil, if a part of that Don Juan were not thereby split off in Leporello, who represents the inner criticism, the anxiety, and the conscience of the hero. With this key we can at last understand why Leporello must represent his master precisely in all the painful situations, and why he is permitted to criticize him and, as it were, to take the place of the conscience that the hero lacks. We can understand, moreover, that the enormity of Don Juan's wickedness is due to the splitting off of the inhibiting element of his personality.

If we consider the plot from this perspective, then we see not only that Leporello clearly represents his master

---

of twenty-three, he wrote to his sister thus: "Laure, Laure, my two solitary and immense desires, to be celebrated and to be loved, shall they ever be satisfied?" [The last two sentences of this paragraph were added in version C. The quotation is from an article, "Feuilleton—Balzac und die Leidenschaft," by E. Curtius, in the *Neue Freie Presse*, April 5, 1922, p. 2. The article is preserved in the Rank papers.]

In a novel by Alexander Arndt that appeared in 1921, *Ti und Tea*, the author not only consciously presents his ego in two independent personalities, but demonstrates himself even more in the subjective connection between these two contrasting figures (see the discussion by Ewald, 1922). [This entire footnote occurs at the end of the previous sentence in Rank's text, but the present location seems more appropriate to me.]

in the scenes already mentioned, but also that he stands for the criticizing and anxiety-oriented conscience of the hero in general. In the first act of the opera he appears as the criticizing agency [of the superego], condemning the dissolute life of his master and acquiescing in it only against his will. Beginning with the scene in the house of Donna Elvira (Act II), where master and servant are at the same time mortally threatened, the guilt feeling comes to the fore. In the cemetery scene and further in the banquet scene, this feeling increases to a terrible anxiety about the ghost of the dead and an unbearable torment of conscience which finally leads to death. If we recognize in Leporello a manifestation—certainly an extraordinarily formed one—of Don Juan's ego ideal, we shall not only be using a formulation of Freud (1914b, 1921), but also approaching a deeper understanding of the whole psychic mechanism.

4.

ELABORATION OF THE
EGO IDEAL

BY the term ego ideal, Freud understood a combination of those criticizing and censoring elements in mankind that normally carry out the repression of certain wishes and that ensure, through a function we call conscience, that these barriers are not broken through. This organ of control in psychic life is composed of two complementary and mutually regulating factors: an outer one, which stands for the demands of the surrounding world; and an inner one, which represents the claims in themselves.[1] More precisely said, the ego ideal is really a representation of inner demands or claims, which have, however, already assimilated the external demands of society. The core of the ego ideal is made up of that part of primary narcissism which the child must renounce in favor of adaptation, but which is preserved in the ego

[1] [I have translated *die Ansprüche* as "claims." In the sense of inner demands, and in contrast with outer demands (*die Forderungen der Umwelt*), the German term is often translated by "aspirations" in English and American psychological usage. Rank is here referring to the two aspects of the ego ideal (external demands and inner aspirations); at this same time, Freud was developing the concept of the "superego" to denote the combination, thus reserving "ego ideal" unambiguously for the aspirations, or inner claims. In this book, I have always translated *Ichideal* as "ego ideal" since Rank never used the term *Überich* (superego), but in some contexts "superego" would be the appropriate contemporary term.]

ideal. The stimulus for the formation of the ego ideal comes from the critical and educational influence of the parents, "to whom were added, as time went on, those who trained and taught him and the innumerable and indefinable host of all the other people in his environment—his fellow-men—and public opinion" (Freud, 1914b, p. 96).

From this point, at which the ego ideal is formed, there is a clear path to the understanding of group psychology which Freud has further pursued in his book, *Group Psychology and the Analysis of the Ego* (1921). Drawing on the phenomena of crowds and groups, he succeeded in showing the roots of the ego ideal in the development of the primal horde, in which the powerful primal father opposed the desires of the sons and acted as an inhibitory principle that was only overcome through actual overthrow and destruction. Before this overthrow was possible, however, the father ruled over the primal horde on the basis of[2] the members' attitude toward him, which Freud characterized as just such a primitive "group formation":

> A primary group of this kind is a number of individuals who have put one and the same object in the place of their ego ideal and have consequently identified themselves with each other in their ego. (1921, p. 116)

This primal connection of the ego ideal with the father figure can also be demonstrated in the development of the individual, where the father becomes the first ideal of the child and, through the mechanism of identification,

[2] [In the original manuscript of *B*, Rank made an interesting slip in repeating this phrase ("auf Grund auf Grund der"), and then correcting the error.]

54

at a certain point becomes an inner claim that fuses with bound-up narcissism to become the ego ideal. We recognize the difficult transitional point of this whole development as the infantile Oedipus complex, which contains the identification with the father in his special role vis-à-vis the mother.

In one place Freud attempts to show the point in man's psychic development where the advance from group psychology to individual psychology took place (1921, pp. 135-36): it occurred after the unsatisfying primal deed—the murder of the father, which brought remorse instead of fulfillment and new complicated inner restrictions instead of the freedom that had been longed for. The advance resulted in fantasy, and the person who made this advance was the first epic poet. This poet distorted the reality in the direction of his own longings. He invented the heroic myth: that it was the hero alone who had slain the father while in fact only the entire horde (the "Band of Brothers") had dared to perform this primal deed. As the father had been the first ideal of the boy, so now the poet created the first ego ideal in the person of the hero who wishes to replace the father. Yet this hero, whose contrived deeds the poet now relates to the multitude, is essentially none other than the poet himself.

If we now look back at the principal male figures of the Don Juan play, we recognize the critical-ironic aspect of the ego ideal in Leporello's clumsy admonitions to reform, while the conscience and guilt feelings of the frivolous hero are split off in Leporello's anxious cowardice. Yet at the decisive tragic high point in the cemetery scene, which introduces the fall of Don Juan, the comic figure of Leporello, who is supposed to deal with the demands of the ego ideal in a mocking way, is cast aside for a far more powerful representative of the ego ideal. This is the consciousness of guilt, and we can readily recognize its representation in the statue of the Commander as a direct father-imago. At the same time, this gradual sharpening and strengthening of the demands of the ego ideal up to the last decisive appearance of the Stone Guest corresponds to an interpretation of the criticizing voice of conscience as the formation of the ideal from the father complex. This psychological elucidation, which is presented in the manner of a dream in the action of the opera itself, can in like manner be traced in the development of the material. In the *Burlador* and in Molière (1665), as well as later in Zorilla (1844), the voice of the cautioner and admonisher devolves directly on the father, toward whom the hero always acts insultingly. In Dorimon (1659) and de Villiers (1660), the immediate predecessors of Molière, it reaches the point of Don Juan's repellent action against his father—as expressed in the title of their plays.[3] In Molière, as also later in his countryman Dumas *père* (1836), it concerns a quarrel about a will, in the course of which the hero shrinks from no crime—not even fratricide—to gain possession of the paternal inheritance.[4] Holtei (1834), who elaborated the material after Mozart, even extended it to parricide: in the course of a chance argument, Don Juan strangles a hermit whom he does not recognize as his father:

[3] Dorimon: *Le festin de Pierre ou le Fils criminel* [The banquet of stone or the criminal son].

[4] [I can find no evidence of such a quarrel, nor of fratricide, in Molière's play, although they occur in Dumas *père*.]

The realization that he had been the slayer of his father made so little an impression on him that immediately after the terrible deed, and in the very hut of the victim, he made a burlesque joke with the coward Leporello. At the end, Don Juan soundly thrashed him. (Heckel, 1915, p. 42)

It is worth noting that in some of the puppet plays[5] the hero also strangles his own father, whereupon the father appears to him as a ghost and dispatches him to hell; for example, in the Ulm and lower Austrian play, *Don Juan der Wilde oder das nächtliche Gericht* [*oder das Steinere Gast*] *oder Junker Hans vom Stein* [Don Juan the wild or the nocturnal meal or the stone guest or Junker Hans of stone].[6]

Here there emerges a significant point which will concern us in the course of our investigation, and which should become understandable in the concluding chapter: that through his transmitting and reworking of the material, the individual poet contributes to it some psychological interpretation, and this interpretation is consistently in accord with the genesis of the material as elucidated through analysis.

[5] [In the manuscript of *B*, Rank deleted the following appositive here: "—whose main contents involve the coarse jokes of Hanswurst or Kasperl, who play the role of Don Juan's servant—". Rank moved this sentence to Chapter 9 in *B*, i.e., from association with explicit parricide to a context suggesting a counterpoise to anxiety and the devaluation of the hero.]

[6] Reported by Kralik and Winter (1885). [Note that "Gericht" can mean either "meal" or "judgment." Rank omits any reference to Shadwell's "The Libertine" (1676), which is probably the best known Don Juan play in which the hero actually kills his own father, perhaps because Heckel gives only brief mention to it.]

Besides the father, it is not unusual for a brother of the hero to be sent from the father to try to bring him to renounce his wicked way of life, as for example in Lenau (1851). In contrast to his predecessors, Lenau has the hero avoid offensive invective, thus raising the conflict to the height of a philosophical discussion of two [different] world views; but in the Don Juan of Dumas *père* referred to above, the conflict leads to a duel between the brothers, during which the brother falls. Don Juan himself dies because the ghost of Sandoval, whom he had also slain in the duel (clearly a further brother-doublet), takes away his life. On the other hand, this Sandoval is an unambiguous double of the hero himself, a "spiritually kindred knight . . . and both are concerned to win over the other the prize for depravity" (Heckel, 1915, p. 55). Here the double relationship is so complete that Sandoval gambles away his beloved to Don Juan, but she dies in order not to become his victim. A similar double motif is found in Zorilla (1844) in the figure of Don Luis Mejia, with whom Don Juan concluded a wager "to surpass him in the number of women seduced and men slain in duels . . . whereupon each can await the other with numbers that provoke astonishment" ([Heckel, 1915, p. 59] see Leporello's "Thousand and Three" aria in *Don Giovanni*). This motif is characteristic of the so-called "lying poems" [*Lügendichtungen*]; some light will be shed on the relationship of these to the Don Juan material later and in another connection.[7]

The close psychological relationship of the double motif to the ego ideal explains why Leporello often ap-

---

[7] It would be worth the effort to treat this topic analytically. The literature can be found in Müller-Fraureuth (1881).

pears as the outspoken double of his master, especially when they represent each other with women (Amphitryon motif:[8] father-identification). The double motif itself certainly seems to correspond to a psychological elaboration of the Don Juan problem. For this reason, we find it only in the more recent Don Juan versions, most clearly in a quite modern one by Sternheim (1909), where an actual double joins himself to the hero as the successor to the servant, who died in the meantime, and accompanies his master till death. By inhibiting the will of his master, whose thirst for action he continually keeps in check with uncanny irony, he is characterized as the critical-ironic part of the ego. As in many of the double stories, this force seems to increase until it reaches the embodiment of madness, in complete agreement with our psychoanalytic interpretation.[9] In contrast to such a "psychologizing" use of the double motif in poetry stands the use of a related motif, which has preserved the original meaning of the double as the messenger of death: namely, the living hero's participation in his own funeral procession. Mérimée (1834) first added this motif to the Don

[8] [Amphitryon had been banished from Argolis as the result of the accidental murder of his wife's father. The wife refused to allow conjugal rights until Amphitryon had avenged the deaths of her brothers. During his absence on a military mission against these enemies, the wife was seduced by Zeus, who had disguised himself as Amphitryon. Heracles was born as the result of this liaison. Amphitryon accepted Heracles as his own son, although some accounts suggest that this was done with reluctance.]

[9] See Rank (1914). [Rank's work on the double (*Der Doppelgänger*) was expanded to a book in 1925, and, like this book, was radically revised after the break with Freud. An English translation of the 1925 German book was published in 1971.]

Juan story when he took over from popular tradition the legend of the knight who saw his own burial and thereafter mended his ways.[10] This motif leads us to the uncanny end of the hero, which is of such surpassing significance in the whole Don Juan tradition.

[10] [Mérimée's work, *Les Âmes du Purgatoire* (The ghosts of purgatory) is based on the cluster of legends associated with Don Miguel de Mañara as discussed in note 11 of Chapter 1, although scholars have found no evidence that Don Miguel actually had such an experience. See Weinstein, 1959, Chapter 10.]

5.

THE FIGURE OF AVENGING
DEATH

We began with a psychological formulation of
the identity or psychic unity of the figures of Don Juan
and Leporello. We believe that this identity can be
viewed as one typical expression of a process of poetic
shaping that results from the formation and artistic representation of the ego ideal. We were able to interpret
these two poetic figures purely in terms of mental[1] mechanisms, because they involve products of artistic fantasy
that spring full-blown from the mind of the poet. However, the figure of the Stone Guest is different. To be sure,
we have interpreted this figure as an ultimate extension
of the series of mental agencies: ego ideal—conscience—
guilt feelings. Yet this does not exhaust the significance
of the figure of the Stone Guest, nor does it fully explain
its origin, for this figure involves an ancient folk-tradition upon which the first poet and creator of Don Juan
drew. Let us read what Heckel says about this tradition:

> Legends of avenging stone statues are already found in
> classical antiquity. Later we find similar fables among
> the most different peoples: French, Portuguese, Flemish,
> German, and Danish folk-traditions all recognize the

[1] [Rank wrote "intrapsychic" mechanisms in the manuscript
of *B*, then changed it to "*seelisch*," which I have translated as
"mental," although in his later work the word tended to con-
note "spiritual." See the translator's introduction to the English
language version of Rank (1930, p. vii).]

story of the skull of a dead man, invited as a guest. Of particular importance is the Leontine Drama that was performed in 1615 at the Jesuit College in Ingolstadt; perhaps a version of this play came to the attention of the author of the *Burlador*.[2] Some comedies of Lope de Vega offer related characteristics: in addition to the *Infamador*, mentioned above, there are *Dineros son Calidad* and *La Fianza Satisfecha*. . . . *The essence of all these representatives is the revenge of the dead man who was mocked, upon the arrogant blasphemer.* (Heckel, 1915, p. 6 [Rank's emphasis])

One can already grasp that the story of the Stone Guest has surpassing significance for the Don Juan material from the fact that it is the subtitle of almost all Don Juan versions. In some versions it is even the main title.

What is the meaning of this motif of avenging death? The conception that the dead return to fetch the living is a very ancient one in human history. Primitive man expressed such a view in his anxiety about the Demons of the Dead, and even in present-day Western culture, "Death" is represented by the figure of a dead person (the skeleton). This significance of fetching by death (as in our "The devil take him!") is fully preserved in the *Burlador*: the Commander appears to Don Juan and invites him to his tomb in a church;[3] the fearless knight accepts this invitation with the result that he does not return. As the folklorist Kleinpaul (1898) has correctly noted, the elementary idea, which is more and more dis-

---

[2] [The careful dating of the composition of the *Burlador* worked out by Wade (1969) makes this almost certainly impossible. See also Weinstein (1959, p. 10).]

[3] [Rank writes *Grabkapelle* (cemetery chapel), but in the *Burlador* this scene takes place at the Commander's tomb, which is located inside a church in Seville.]

torted over time, is that the dead man kills his murderer. In the *Burlador* this primitive notion is employed with good taste in a flippant way when Don Juan pledges his faithfulness to Aminta. He swears that if he betrays her, then a man should kill him—at the same time whispering, "A dead man, certainly not a living one!" by which he believes that he has annulled his oath. In later versions, the Commander appears only as a messenger of death who announces to Don Juan that he will die on the following morning. This sense of the interpretation of the motif, however, can only suggest that the magnificent final scene means that Don Juan is taken by death, therefore dies, and that in his last hours his previously suppressed conscience awakens. Such an explanation is banal, for it neither satisfies our intellectual interest nor makes understandable the terrifying effect of the scene on the audience,[4] especially if we do not further investigate the traces of a connection between anxiety about death and feelings of guilt that are intimated here.

This strong effect of the final scene is, moreover, not further clarified by the simple reflection that the figure of "Death coming to get the living" stirs up one of the oldest and deepest human emotions. More than twenty-five years ago, Kleinpaul (1898) pointed out the great significance for cultural history of the belief in physical, embodied ghosts, closely connected with the corpse and its process of decay. Naumann (1921) quite recently indicated the wide range of material suggesting that countless customs, forms, and motifs are based on a kind of materialistic pre-animism, although it is remark-

---

[4] [Rank here introduces the psychoanalytic issue of the motives behind the reaction of the audience, in addition to the motives behind the creation of the poet. The first issue is pursued in Holland (1968).]

able that he made no reference to his predecessor Klein-paul. Naumann sees as the basis of such "non-spiritual" beliefs:

> that with the onset of death, a man certainly does not lose the features of his living body, as happens with the departure of the soul, according to the belief in souls. He only withdraws from the community of living persons into that of the uncanny, superhuman, and demonic. (p. 23)

Only with the process of decay do significant changes occur in the body. These lead to a second death, according to a widespread notion that was still real in the Homeric world with its rather naive and simple belief in souls. Even after this second death due to decay, however, there survives a further entity which is reflected in the Greek conception of the soul, as well as in our own folk-belief about the Grim Reaper. Anxiety about this dead person who lives on, materially or immaterially, gives rise to a series of customs which can be understood as measures of protection against the return of the dead person:

> A crouched position, the binding and swathing of the dead, placing in narrow boxes and holes, piling up enormous stones and earth, and finally the hidden underground grave and so forth are today rightly understood as measures of protection and defense by the living against the dead. The intention of preventing their return is the principal answer (and perhaps the only one) to the question about the original cause of burying the dead, a practice that is demanded by the relentless strength of popular feeling. (Naumann, 1921, p. 57)

In this connection, Naumann also conceives the custom of burning the corpse, which appeared later, as an advanced rite of defense; yet the failure of this defense is betrayed in the extensiveness and tenacity of animistic beliefs in souls.

Here often in the history of a scientific idea, the emphasis upon what had been previously disregarded leads to the other extreme. While Naumann rightly emphasized as an explanatory principle the immediate, tangible, perceivable appearances of the physical world as against the over-valuation of later animism, he lost sight of the psychological element itself—that which in the last analysis is a legitimate descendant of animism.[5] As a result, the whole problem of the belief in a dead person who continues a material existence, and the *anxiety* that this belief arouses, remain psychologically unexplained. Here the author obviously lacks the psychoanalytic point of view toward the understanding of the belief in demons that Freud gave us in *Totem and Taboo* (1913). For men come to the conception of anxiety which persists in the cult of the dead only because of guilt feelings that extend back to the ambivalence of the Oedipus complex. Only because of these guilt feelings do they thus view dying as the revenge of the dead; that is, that natural death, which in primitive times was not natural, is felt as punishment. This psychoanalytic interpretation presupposes that death was understood as the act of a murdered person who in turn had to avenge his own murder, a conception in which the primitive situation survives.

Such an interpretation explains why among many peoples the death of a person is always understood to be the

[5] [Rank developed this theme in *Psychology and the Soul* (1930).]

act of revenge of a murdered man; and that while living humans cannot accomplish such revenge by natural means, the dead can do so through demons. As Naumann reports, Indian folktales clearly assert that men undergo a transition into demons through the medium of death. "The ascetic dies with the intention of bloodily avenging himself and would become a Rakshasa,[6] that is, a demon, vampire, or dragon" (Naumann, 1921, p. 51). Or a person takes his own life in order to be able to carry out particular threats. This is a magical motif that plays a role that should not be underestimated in the psychology of suicide,[7] in which the suicide revenges himself on those whom he believes to have caused his misfortune.[8]

If we put together the psychoanalytic understanding of the belief in demons with another characteristic of these dangerous corpses that also has not been previously understood, then it is possible to reconstruct a further piece of primitive history. This in turn makes understandable the legend of the avenging corpse in the particular form that it takes in Don Juan. This characteristic is the belief that the corpse-demon frequently devours those living persons who have the misfortune to be caught by him, a belief illustrated in the rich material of Naumann and even Kleinpaul. Naumann cites a great

[6] [*Rakshasas* were demon powers of evil and enemies of the gods in Hindu legends. They had sexual relations with humans, and delighted in destroying people and drinking their blood. According to one account, the Rakshasas originated from the rebellious, cannibalistic sons of the god Brahma (Thomas, 1961, p. 13). Ravana, who was a Rakshasa, abducted Sita (the wife of Rama) and thus precipitated the battle described in the *Ramayana* epic.]

[7] According to Indian popular belief, wishes uttered immediately before suicide are fulfilled. See Hertel (1921, p. 249).

[8] [The last clause is added in version G.]

number of such traditions from different peoples, though of course they are not understood or explained:

> If a dead Fiji warrior falls in battle against the monster Samu, then the monster boils and devours him; thus both demon and warrior are thought of in strictly material terms, for otherwise boiling and eating a soul would hardly be worth the effort. The case of Samu also involves the appearance of the corpse who devours, as do the Nordic tales (Hräswelgr, Nidhöggr), the Chinese tales, and many other forms. (:921, p. 29)

In Chinese tales, the profaner of graves who opens the heavy coffin the slightest bit is then pulled in by the dead person, torn to pieces, and devoured. From this belief we can explain a whole series of death customs, including that of the parting gift of food for the later "journey into the hereafter":

> Thus Nordic corpses in mound-graves devour hawks, dogs, and horses that have been given to them. . . . The mouth of the corpse should not remain open, for otherwise the dead will have no peace in the grave and will become *Nachzehrers*.[9] The edges of clothing should not come too near his mouth, otherwise he will become a nachzehrer. . . . And these Chinese and Nordic devourers in the coffin and grave are closely related to the German and Slavic belief in nachzehrers, bloodsuckers,

[9] [*Nachzehrer* means, literally, "after-devourer." It is a German variant of the vampire. It "sucks and feeds on its own clothes and limbs in the grave, and extracts the vital energy of related family members through a form of sympathetic magic acting at a distance" (*Brockhaus Enzyklopädie*, 17th edition, 1971). Because there seems to be no precise equivalent term in English, and because I think that the word *nachzehrer* has a certain vividness, I have used the German term.]

and vampires. Even the belief in vampires rests on wholly pre-animistic conceptions. Corpses with fresh coloring and open left eyes keep themselves alive in the grave, come out at night, suck the blood of their victims, and quickly take away their family and later the whole village community. The ancient belief is especially active during times of severe plague. If one exhumed the nachzehrer, one found him swimming in blood, and torn and scratched to pieces. Perhaps from the struggle with the victim, which one cannot represent tangibly enough. . . . The first person affected and killed by the plague becomes the vampire; he sits upright in his grave and feeds on his shroud. The plague lasts as long a time as he takes to be finished with it. The nachzehrer is disinterred and his head is cut off with a spade, so that he "screams like a young pig." (Naumann, 1921, pp. 55, 41, 55-56)

Kleinpaul at least makes an attempt to understand these remarkable characteristics attributed to the dead; and if he views them "rationally," at least he intelligently indicates the deeper relationships, and in the end recognizes the consequence that cannibalism plays an important role. In primitive times, the main food of men would have been other men, and this deeply-rooted fact still survives today in many rudimentary forms, including the legend of the werewolf (Kleinpaul, 1898, p. 122). With support from prehistorical and ethnological discoveries, Kleinpaul at one point even ventures to assert that the devouring of the dead:

is the oldest and most widespread form of human obsequies for the dead. Thus it may be noted that the custom of themselves consuming the dead bodies of their fellows,[10] and burying the bones, has been observed among many people and even among higher animals. W. M. Flinders Petrie found carefully arranged human bones, suggesting an artistic dismemberment of the skeleton, in many Egyptian stone graves dating from the Fourth Millennium B.C.[11] Some were in coffins; some wrapped in simple shrouds. As a result of the discovery, he was led to ascribe this custom, called *endocannibalism*, to the ancient Egyptians (1898, p. 63).

When such a manner of disposal was felt to be too repulsive, this heritage of primitive humanity was left to *animals*; and thereby arose a taboo which for thousands of years has made irreconcilable the gap between man and the animals related to him. In Egypt, it was evidently the vulture, who plays such a great role in the traditions of that culture that have come down to us; in other lands, various kinds of dogs and carnivorous animals of the dog family (jackals, wolves, hyenas, etc.). The custom of abandoning the dead as food for certain animals is preserved down to the present day among many peoples. The Parsis, descendants of the ancient Persians, take their dead to the "Towers of Silence"[12] where, ac-

[10] [*Angehörigen*. Version *G*, has "parents" as, presumably, a translation of Kleinpaul!]

[11] How insignificant are these historical dates in the face of the prehistoric skeleton discoveries that attest to cannibalism in prehistoric Europe! As an example, one notes that Otto Hauser concluded from the find at Krapina (in Croatia) that anthropophagy [the eating of humans] stood in full flower about 40,000 years ago (*Urmensch und Wilder*. Berlin: Verlag Ullstein & Co., 1921).

[12] [These towers are located in Bombay, where a majority of the Parsi community have lived for the past several hundred years, after migrating from Persia.]

cording to the ancient precepts of the *Avesta*,[13] they are then set out and abandoned as prey for the birds. Kleinpaul convincingly demonstrates that the official devourer of corpses among the Persians was originally the dog, an animal that nowadays plays only a mute role in the ceremony (1898, p. 62).[14] The Parsi is supposed to die while in the sight of a dog who has been brought into the room of the dying person in order to strike the fleeing soul with his glance.

> In order to direct the gaze of the dog to [the dead person], a loaf of bread is cut up into four pieces and thrown in the direction of the death-bed. Western scholars are here reminded of the honey cake, the *Melitouta*, which was once laid next to the corpse for the Cerberus[15] in Greece. . . . This ceremony is called the *Sägdid*—literally: the dog (Säg) has seen (did). It is the endorsement of the holy animal, the *Vidimus des Todes* [We have seen the dead]. (1898, p. 59)

The ceremony is then repeated in the conveying of the dead person to the tower, and as soon as the dog has seen the face of the dead person for the second time, the body is left as food. Originally, the dog was to eat the corpse himself just like the Cerberus, who lets everyone in but no one out—a real watchman, as in the well-known passage of [Hesiod's] *Theogony:*

> On those [dead] who go in he fawns with his tail and both his ears, but suffers them not to go out back again,

[13] [The *Avesta* is the original document of Zoroastrianism, from which the Parsis descend.]

[14] Herodotus actually says of the Persians that no corpse could be buried until a dog or bird had torn at it [*Histories*, I, 140].

[15] [A monstrous dog that guarded the entrance to the lower world.]

but keeps watch and devours whomsoever he catches going out of the gates.[16]

Kleinpaul acutely comprehends that this "dog of hell" was the corpse dog who had been banished from the underworld because his earthly duty had become taboo. He draws a parallel to the vulture, who was banished to the underworld by the Greeks in the same way, and who while there devoured the liver of the giant Tytus, a torment of hell that the mythic Prometheus also suffered for his crime of stealing fire. "The terrors of the underworld are drawn from the burial customs of earthly life" (Kleinpaul, 1898, p. 88). Thus the Christian hell consisted of a confluence of individual funeral pyres into one mighty stream of fire, a fire that cuts off any return journey and, finally, is an all-encircling prison of flames for the souls of the damned, who are thereby immortal even as they suffer the eternal torments of hell.

Among primitive peoples who have not developed such an elaborate mythology, we find the customs for disposal of the dead at a still earlier stage of development. Thus according to the latest report of Hermann Consten,[17] who travelled in Asia, the Mongolians of the Gobi Desert believe in a process of rebirth, which they would have the dead participate in as quickly as possible. Nevertheless, the arrangements that they prepare for it seem to us an effective way of preventing any possibility of rebirth. Usually the corpses are abandoned as food for dogs. Near large lakes they are thrown into the water

[16] [English translation by H. G. Evelyn-White (Loeb Classical Library edition); lines 769 ff.]

[17] [Probably based on a newspaper account of Consten's travels, "Barbarische Totenbräuche," in the *Neues Wiener Journal*, February 7, 1922, p. 5. The article is preserved in the Rank papers. See also Consten (1919).]

to be destroyed by the fish. In high places they are ex-
posed on a bundle of sticks or on the bare rocks as food
for the vultures. Consten had the opportunity of attend-
ing the funeral of a distinguished lama, and from his description we shall give special attention to the drum and
trumpet music. The double drums were made out of two
pieces of wood, covered with stretched human skin. Human vertebrae and other bones were attached to these
drums, so that with the rapid whirling movements of the
drummers' wrists, the bones struck the drum with great
force. The trumpets were likewise fashioned out of hol-
low human bones. These features of the musical instru-
ments suggest that the original function of "music" is to
be found in rites of mourning.[18]

[18] Here we refer only to the well-known Biblical legend of
the invention of the lute: The first person to use the lute was
Lamech [Lamek], who descended in a direct line from Adam.
This Lamech had a son whom he loved dearly. As death took
his son from him, he suspended the body from a tree. The
joints fell apart, and there remained only the thigh and its
bones, and the foot with toes. Lamech took a piece of wood,
cut and polished it, and made a lute from it. He gave the instrument the shape of a thigh, and in each part of its construction
he imitated the remaining bones of his son. Then he sang a
song of mourning. This Lamech founded a whole family of musicians; his son Tubal invented the drums, and his daughter
Julal the harp.

[This note was added in version C. Although I have searched
Biblical reference works, reference works on Jewish legends
and traditions, and music reference works—all in English and
German—I am unable to find any trace of such a legend.

The only mention of Lamech in the Old Testament occurs
in Genesis 4:17-24. Lamech was a fifth-generation descendant
from Cain; he had two wives (the earliest Biblical reference
to polygamy), three sons (Jabal, Jubal, and Tubal-cain) and
one daughter (Naamah). He sang a song of blood revenge:

Yet our own "civilized" burial customs are no more distant from their primitive precursors than we ourselves are from the men who practiced them. First, there is the fact that we also let our dead be devoured by maggots and worms, creatures that Kleinpaul classed among the carrion eaters (1898, p. 73). Then there is the grave itself, which derives from the belief in the soul, and was devised as a way of preventing carrion eaters from completely destroying the body. Yet the grave itself has become regarded as the symbol of one such carrion eater: our word "Sarg" [coffin] derives from the Greek *sarcophagos*, which literally means "flesh-eater" (Kleinpaul,

---

Adah and Zillah, listen to me;
wives of Lamech, mark what I say:
I kill a man for wounding me,
a young man for a blow.
Cain may be avenged seven times,
but Lamech seventy-seven. (*New English Bible*)

One Talmudic legend goes beyond this revenge song to suggest that while hunting with his son Tubal-cain, the aged and blind Lamech accidentally killed his ancestor Cain. Upon discovering this, he clapped his hands, and this act killed Tubal-cain. Thereupon his wives deserted him. One source adds that Lamech in fact killed no one; but that his wives refused to associate with him because of their fear that all descendants of Cain would be destroyed after seven generations. This source has Lamech saying to the wives "Have I slain man or youth that my offspring should be destroyed? If Cain can expiate his crime after seven generations, surely Lamech, who killed no one, shall expiate his sins after seventy-seven generations" (From *The Jewish Encyclopedia*, 1904 edition).

There are other Biblical references to this Lamech story; and an additional reference in Genesis to a Lamech who was the father of Noah. Scholars are not certain whether this is a different Lamech or the same one.]

1898, pp. 70f). As Pliny reports, the Greeks actually derived this word from the very corrosive characteristic of the caustic substance that apparently was often used in sarcophagi. However, Kleinpaul argues plausibly enough that this etymological myth originated to account for the incomprehensibility of the "flesh-eating" grave itself (p. 77).[19] As a symbol of the vengeance of hell that devours humans, the stone sarcophagus appears in *Hamlet* as a simile:

> Why the sepulchre
> Wherein we saw thee quietly interred
> Hath oped his ponderous and marble jaws
> To cast thee up again. (Hamlet to his father's ghost;
> act 1, scene 4, 48-51)

Probably this symbolic aspect plays a great part in the meaning of the Stone Guest figure, which itself personifies the devouring grave. Such a symbolic connection appears in the strict sense that the "rigidity, coldness, and weight of the corpse is, through unbounded fantasy, transformed into stone," as Naumann thought (1921, pp. 42f.). Yet if we ask about the psychological motive for this particular conception [of the Stone Guest as the devouring grave], we see the operation of the guilt and punishment tendencies, since the stone statue set near the dead person represents the grave that one day will devour everyone. The interpretation of the stone tomb as

[19] [Kleinpaul argues that while corrosive quicklime acts in such a way, "eating away" the flesh from the skeleton just as a dog would do, nevertheless the tomb or stone coffin itself has the opposite property: it does not corrode. Thus the phrase "flesh-eating" in reference to this non-corrosive stone must be a symbol for the overall "swallowing up" connotation of the grave.]

punishment possibly conceals a vestige of an early method of killing. Roheim alludes to this possibility in his observation that among primitive men the stone represented both a deadly murder weapon at a distance and also, at the grave, a barrier to the return of the murdered person.[20] Certain customs relating to death still appear to have this double sense, which can be conceptualized as the "stoning of the dangerous spirit"—a custom that is familiar in the area around Mecca (Kleinpaul, 1898, p. 64). The motif also appears in a Chinese tale (#69 in Wilhelm, 1914) as an action of revenge by the dead: the living corpse comes out of his grave and, in the person of an ill-bred youth, throws stones at the living.

For a further understanding of the Stone Guest, we draw upon the traditions of demon corpses who devour men. These traditions also involve the motif of *invitation*. "One variation of the stone man is the iron or partly-iron man." Balkan Tale #59 (in Leskien, 1915) introduces the partly-iron demon who devours men—he smells human flesh and sucks the blood from the new arrival. "The Wolf with the Iron Head" of Balkan Tale #63 (in Leskien, 1915) is a dangerous demon. The tale is about a man-eating creature who according to his promise returns on the day of the marriage in order to take away the bridegroom. The man-eating iron dervish of the modern Greek Tale #60 (in Kretschmer, 1917)

[20] In his paper "Steinheiligtum und Grab" presented at a meeting of the Budapest Psychoanalytic Society on October 8, 1921: "Stone-throwing in religious rites is a relic of the primal struggle of mankind. The thrown stone was the characteristic weapon of the masses, in order to overpower the individual in whose close presence one did not venture." [See Roheim, 1921.]

The punishment interpretation of piles of stones is preserved in the Israelite custom of piling up stones over the body of an executed criminal. (See Georg Beer, 1921.)

from Epirus is an exact parallel in purer form. However, the purest version of the motif is shown in the modern Icelandic legend of "The Bridegroom and the Ghost." Here also the demon, "a fearfully large man," appears on the day of the wedding to which he had been invited in jest five years before by the bridegroom, a young grave-digger, as he turned up a huge thigh bone while digging a grave (Naumann, 1921, p. 44; see also the cemetery scene in *Hamlet* [act 5, scene 1]!).

Thus we have approached a first understanding of the motif of the Stone Guest, who also appears in response to a flippant invitation in order to take the living away with him. The anxiety of those who are to be devoured appears to be reworked, through the mocking Don Juan character of the opera, into a mirthful banquet,[21] a kind of Feast of the Dead, in which the dead person himself should participate.[22] In the *Burlador*, the Stone Guest

[21] [In Act 2, Scene 6 of *Don Giovanni*, the statue appears at the banquet to which he has been invited just after the hero concludes a toast with the words: "Long live women, long live good wine! Sustenance and glory of humanity!"]

[22] In a similar way, Prince Hamlet also philosophized in a famous passage:

King: Now, Hamlet, where's Polonius?
Hamlet: At supper.
King: At supper! Where?
Hamlet: Not where he eats, but where he is eaten: a certain convocation of politic worms are e'en at him. Your worm is your only emperor for diet: we fat all creatures else to fat us, and we fat ourselves for maggots: your fat king and your lean beggar is but variable service, two dishes, but to one table: that's the end. (Act 4, scene 3, 17-27.)

In the Hamlet legend, the motif is still preserved in its original form, as the hero, after killing the eavesdropper to the con-

actually sits silently at the table while the others around him try to stifle their inner terror through redoubled exuberance. And at the tomb in the church, where he has come in response to the Commander's invitation, Don Juan is compelled to eat dishes of scorpions and serpents, to drink bitter vinegar as wine, and to hear songs of lament as dinner music. After the meal, the sentence of judgment is fulfilled—a judgment that Don Juan brought upon himself when he affirmed in making a promise of marriage, "If my word is the least bit false, may the hand of a dead man destroy me!" In this frightening hand of the corpse, threatening from the grave, we recognize the expression of an ineradicable feeling of guilt in the presence of the dreaded paternal punishment.

---

versation with his mother, dismembers him and then throws him to the pigs as fodder. (See the motif of dismemberment in the next chapter.)

6.

THE PRIMAL FATHER AND AVENGING DEATH

If WE believe that the legend of the flesh-eating Demon of Death who avenges the primal crime can be recognized in the Stone Guest figure of the Don Juan legend, then the question is raised of how such an interpretation is related both to our previous explanation of the figure as conscience and also to the Don Juan motif itself. We shall find the answers to both questions in human prehistory and its vestiges in the later traditions.

The demon of death, who returns from the grave to devour the guilty, is nothing other than the personification of the pangs of conscience, which as such betray their origin in the primal act of parricide. The anxiety about the return of the father and his particular revenge (devouring), which is reduced by the different burial customs, can be explained as anxiety about retaliation, arising from a sense of guilt. The totem meal, which Freud's interpretation has illuminated as a theme that survives in the idea of sacrificial food, the Last Supper ("Take and eat; this is my body"), and the funeral banquet, ultimately finds its prehistoric prototype in the devouring of the father who was collectively slain. Such an hypothesis, which appears repellent to our sensitivities, is confirmed not only by the fact of cannibalism, but by a series of very special ethnological customs. Thus Herodotus (*Histories*, III, 38) reports that the Callatiae (an Indian people) eat their fathers. Among the Massagetae (I, 216), relatives kill a person who grows very old along "with beasts of the flock besides, then they boil the flesh and feast on it. This is held to be the best sort of death."[1] One can try to render these customs more understandable if one recognizes that they are based on deeply rooted superstitions that survive in religion.[2] Primitive man consumes certain parts of an animal in order to appropriate its strength. He also believes that he appropriates the powers of the mighty primal father for himself in the same way, by eating certain parts of the body. Any anxiety that the slain person might return to avenge his murder is, moreover, quite effectively checked by the radical manner of his destruction, and also by the identification that is symbolized by eating.[3] Of course, neither the destruction nor the identification through eating achieves the intended result, for at this point there emerges a sense of guilt that cannot be placated. For while the primitive death rite achieves the quickest possible destruction of the body by means of eating (although not without leaving some traces), it also creates and strengthens an immaterial, mysterious sense of guilt. In the mythic and religious traditions, this

[1] Among many peoples even today, the custom of killing aged people to rid oneself of them survives, as among the Eskimo and the natives of Greenland. In the latter case, if the father is old and of no use, the son takes him and hangs him. Among the Chippewa of North America, the father is ejected from the home. [In version G Rank adds Koty (1934) as a reference here.] That the son has this duty of doing away with his frail and infirm father among so many peoples can only be understood as a conscious echo of the death sacrifice.

[2] Hirsch (1922) gives a psychological description of food aversions.

[3] Cf. the "oral" dependence aspect of identification (Freud, 1921, p. 105f.).

guilt feeling continually seeks exoneration and justification, even when the body of the slain person is completely and utterly annihilated by fire, the sense of guilt finds no peace. For the eternally living sense of guilt even allows the body to be "devoured" by the flames, and through this process of material refining the detached "soul" is set free. This soul persists as the invisible enemy in the animistic superstition, as it does in the neurotic symptoms until it is transmuted into scientific consciousness by psychoanalysis.

From one of the early phases of the primordial struggle against this materialized conscience, a series of Greek myths is derived in which the motif of *dismembering* is closely related to that of killing and devouring of men. Because I have already discussed these traditions—of Pelops, Atreus, Thyestes, Harpagos, and others—in another place (Rank, 1912, pp. 283-97, 309-19 especially), I am content to note here that they characteristically involve children who are set as food before the father. The Greek cosmology of Cronos, who devoured his children and who was castrated by his youngest son Zeus,[4] dis-

[4] [Cronos, at the urging of his mother Gaia ("Earth"), castrated his father Uranos ("Heaven") while the latter approached Gaia. This was in revenge for Uranos' having hid all his children in the huge body of Gaia. The phallus of Uranos was thrown into the sea; from the foam that gathered about it sprang Aphrodite. (Hesiod, *Theogony*, lines 145-210; Rose, 1953, p. 22 summarizes the account together with variations.)

Later, Cronos produced children with his consort Rhea and swallowed them as fast as they were born. Rhea hid Zeus and in his place gave Cronos a stone wrapped in swaddling clothes to swallow. Upon reaching maturity, Zeus fought against his father Cronos. Rhea caused Cronos to vomit forth his swallowed children, and Zeus set free certain of his father's brethren who had been imprisoned by Cronos (Rose, 1953, pp. 32-44). In an

places the tradition to a prehistoric era but reproduces it in its full, unretouched crudeness.[5] Yet the Cronos myth is a heroic revision of the Egyptian Osiris myth, which at certain points is more primitive. In this myth, Osiris, who is sexually favored by his sister Isis, is killed by his brother acting together with a number of helpers (14 or 26 or 72 [according to different versions]). They divide the body of Osiris into the appropriate number of pieces. According to Diodor,[6] the brother gives a piece of the body of Osiris to each of his 26 accomplices in order to diminish their individual guilt; but no one will take the phallus—clearly the symbol of principal guilt. As a very special part of the body, this also has a special fate: it is permanently lost, the underlying intention[7] being that a fish should devour it. Meanwhile the sense of guilt, in the form of a fantasied wish, brings all of the remaining parts together into a whole body again—as often occurs in stories of this type. Perhaps this compensatory reaction to primitive dismemberment preserves the mythic expression of a step of cultural evolution, in

---

earlier work (Rank, 1912, p. 269), Rank argues that this standard account of Zeus and Cronos is a distortion of the original version, which survives in the Orphic Theogony (Preller, 1887, I, p. 56, note 3), where Cronos is castrated by Zeus in the same way that Cronos castrated Uranos. Rank argues that the change was made because of the heightened anxiety about retaliation.]

[5] According to Naumann's interpretation (1921, p. 70), the child-eater theme even appears in the Herod figure of the Jesus tradition. It survives and is further rationalized in the story of Ugolino related by Dante (canto 33 of *The Inferno*); while Gerstenberg dealt with it in a tragedy where the father, who is starving in a tower, feeds off the bodies of his children.

[6] [*The Library of History of Diodorus of Sicily* (Diodorus Siculus, Book I, Chapter 21.]

[7] [The intention, conscious or unconscious, presumably, of the person who lost it.]

which the Egyptians moved from devouring their dead to the reverent custom of embalming, which protects that very corpse from "being devoured" chemically.

The theme of the many collaborators in the primal crime appears in the earliest traces of the Osiris myth. In the later hero myths, these collaborators are absent and are replaced by one person—the youngest [of them]— who often plays the role of the aristocratic braggart [*Junker Prahlhans*] in our [German language] stories. By comparing the Egyptian Osiris legend with the Greek Cronos myth, we can apprehend the entire course of the heroic re-working of the original material, although we are convinced that the Egyptian version does not reproduce the primordial history unchanged. In the Osiris version, the primal father [figure] was attacked by the horde for reasons of sexual jealousy; he was dismembered and, we may suppose, devoured. In the later traditions this dismemberment happens only to the phallus. In the Greek version, the father god is deceived during the sex act and only castrated (the phallus is thrown into the sea), for the noteworthy reason that "he first thought of doing shameful things" (*Theogony*, lines 167-68). This reason alludes to the father's suspecting the danger in his sons and either preventing their birth or else devouring them immediately after birth. Here we find the first hint of justification of the primal crime against the father, that he was reproached with having devoured his own sons. This need for justification—in connection with the role of the woman in the heroic tradition [see Chapter 7]—leads us to conclude, with Freud, that heroic poetry is in fact a false re-working of reality in the sense that it is a fantasied wish.[8]

[8] [See Freud (1921, pp. 135-36). In the *Theogony*, the mother gives this "justification."]

As the most widely known example of this total reversal in fantasy, we mention the numerous stories of ogres found among both primitive and civilized peoples. The story is familiar to us as the popular Tom Thumb [*Däumling*] tale. Tom Thumb and his brothers were cast out of their parents' house. In the wild forest, they came toward evening to the house of a giant ogre who was not at home. His sympathetic wife hid them. When the giant came home, he scented the prey with the well-known exclamation, "I smell human flesh!" With some effort, the wife was able to gain a respite until the next morning for her charges. During the night, however, the monster came into the bedroom to cut the throats of the seven brothers. Because of a cunning trick of Tom Thumb, he killed his own seven daughters instead. The brothers fled. Tom Thumb took the Seven-League Boots of the ogre with him, an act which corresponds not only to a castration of the primal father, but also to an identification with him. This version has preserved a trace of the transformation [of the original], in that the youngest son is set off from the horde of brothers in the shape of a phallus (Tom Thumb); the more usual story tradition indicates that only *one* person, the hero, is concealed and "saved" by the woman in the same way as the phallus was concealed and "saved" by the loving goddess Isis.[9] That the fantasy does not take offense at such an ignominious role for the hero is explained by the sexual motivation that is symbolically displayed in this fantasy—

[9] [Isis wished Osiris to be honored by the Egyptians, and so she reconstituted his body. According to Diodor, she fashioned the figure of a human body from each of the various fragments, and had these artificial bodies buried in various localities. Thinking the phallus especially worthy, she had images of it made for the temples. See also Rank (1913).]

breaking in, concealment by the woman, and deception of the giant. We still have to consider the role of the woman; here we only want to suggest that the whole fantasy recalls the Freudian interpretation, whereby:

> in the lying poetic fancies of prehistoric times the woman, who had been the prize of battle and the temptation to murder, was probably turned into the active seducer and instigator to the crime. (Freud, 1921, p. 136)

Concerning the origin and role of the ogre, we consider Naumann (1921, p. 45) wrong when, in agreement with Schoning (1903), he explains the giant as a corpse-demon, enlarged by fantasy to the proportions of a giant. Clearly, the psychological connection between the demon and the giant can only be that both are personifications of the all-powerful, brutal primal father. In both forms he is essentially dangerous; the difference is only that the corpse-demon who devours the living appears to the guilt feelings of the murderers as revenging his own "feast," while the giant ogre corresponds to a justification fantasy of the hero, who pretends to expiate an earlier crime of the father by means of the primal act ("He first thought of doing shameful things").

We can instruct ourselves about the further meaning of this ogre fantasy, and especially about the role played by the woman, by drawing on similar traditions of primitive peoples as collected by Frobenius (1904). The role of the woman as helper—often completely without motivation—is usually explained by her being the wife (or sister) of the hero, who had previously been abducted by the giant and who is now possessed by him. The hero sets out to rescue her from the power of the primal father, so that his action is justified (as for example among the Tibetan Mongols, in the fourth chapter of the *Bogda Gesser Chan*).[10] According to Frobenius, the death of the ogre (giant) occurs either through the swallowing of white-hot stones (as we know from the Cronos myth and the story of Little Red Riding Hood),[11] through turning to stone (the Stone Guest of the Don Juan legend), or through dismembering (the devouring motif). Frobenius also includes here the Indo-European Polyphemus legend. He characterizes this ogre-type in a way that fully corresponds to our analytical reconstruction: Ogres are cave-dwellers, who have a definite temporal place in the history of the origin of the world. Often they appear as a group, although the hero usually struggles with only one. Always there is only *one* woman. Generally, she does not belong to the race of ogres, since she helps the hero who is sheltered in the cave—often even to the point of killing the ogres. In the end, this "old helper,"[12] as Frobenius calls her, turns out to be the mother of the hero (for example in Lapland); but if she

[10] [*Die Taten Bogda Gesser Chan* (The acts of Bogda Gesser Chan) is a religious heroic saga of the Tibetan Mongols. The German translation of 1839 by I. J. Schmidt was reissued by the Auriga Verlag, Berlin, in 1925. Rank doubtless knew of the book through Frobenius's work. Poppe (1926) gives further information about the book.]

[11] [It will be recalled that the original German version of this fairy tale (*Rottkäppchen*) has Red Riding Hood swallowed by the wolf. A hunter later hears the wolf snoring and, thinking that he has devoured the grandmother, cuts open the wolf's stomach with a scissors. Red Riding Hood and the grandmother appear out of the open stomach, and they put stones into the wolf's belly. When the wolf awakes, he tries to run away, but the stones are so heavy that he collapses and falls dead. See Grimm and Grimm (1837) for the original German, and Hunt (1944) for a literal English translation.]

[12] [*"Hilfsalte."* Version G has "good old woman."]

is young, then the hero carries her off as a virginal maid and marries her.

According to our hypothesis, this mythical role of the woman cannot have been the original one. The legendary wishful fantasy (in Freud's sense) presupposes that the sexual object was already bound to the heroic youngest son as a helper, while in fact she was first obtained with difficulty through the removal of the old man. Originally, the woman apparently had to be subdued, just like the jealous father; for after his murder she would obviously protect the freedom that she had thereby won. Thus we can explain the fact that in some isolated traditions, the woman who became the "old helper" of the hero myths appears as a partisan of the giants. Here she is herself an ogre who summons her mate to devour the hero-guest.[13] This "bad old woman" survives in the figure of the Devil's grandmother[14] and also in the Raven Mother of so many mythic traditions. Her role in stories has become that of the witch or the bad stepmother. But how did the mother take on this hostile role?

[13] According to Frobenius (1904, p. 382), the female cannibal is prominent especially among the German tribes of Europe, among the Italians, and among the Africans both north and south; while the ogre predominates everywhere in the East, he is a figure that comes and goes in the West.

[14] [The German term, *Ellermutter*, means grandmother or great-grandmother.]

7.

THE DON JUAN LEGEND AS
HEROIC DISTORTION

We have certainly come rather far from the
theme of Don Juan and his adversary the Stone Guest,
but we have moved in the direction of the heroic legends
of prehistory because we can regard the Don Juan fantasy as their most extreme development. Don Juan is the
audacious blasphemer, who would deny conscience,
guilt feelings, and anxiety with a cynicism that surpasses
anything in the heroic tradition. He stifles his dread of
the flesh-eating primal father's revenge with an unelicited
invitation to a mirthful banquet. Yet on the other hand,
he openly admits the primal crime; according to our interpretation, this must be contrasted to the otherwise
heroic portrait. Freed from all burden of guilt, the Don
Juan figure can permit himself, as it were, to acknowl-
edge the primitive instinctual roots of the primal crime
without extenuating motives. He can admit, moreover,
that the father was murdered for reasons of base sensuality rather than from a desire to rescue the beloved
woman from oppression.

Thus the surpassing greatness of the Don Juan figure
is that he has done away with the heroic lie. He removes
the men in order to possess the women. He knows no
ideal motives, no sentimentalities and rationalizations. He
has preserved the heroic character only in the one essential point that keeps him from being identified as a common criminal: he stands *alone*—alone against a world of

opponents, and alone against an underworld full of dangers. As in the case of the heroic poet, he cannot use the help of brothers in the primal deed. He will not divide the booty of women with them afterwards, but rather will possess each one for himself alone. Each time anew he overcomes another awesome primal father, who had not permitted any higher stage of social organization.[1] His tragedy, and finally his death, come from this complete identification with the tyrannical father; for he himself is now pursued by the steadily growing band of avengers, just as the primal father was pursued by the horde [of brothers]. Finally he succumbs to the narcissistically determined anxiety about retaliation which always arises from such an identification.

Now in terms of the heroic fantasy portrait, it is noteworthy that the very point that makes our hero a hero, and that constitutes his special characteristic, also causes him to slip into the lying exaggeration of the typical story hero. He does establish the individual, heroic ego —the ego ideal—for the horde of brothers; and while he does not multiply and exaggerate the primal deed, as do the ancient heroes in their heroic deeds, he does exaggerate and multiply his desired success—the number of women of the primal horde whom he conquers. The thousand and three women whom he substitutes for the one conquered woman of the heroic myths betray the

---

[1] Thus as Schmitz (1913) notes, Don Juan can only exist in a country where the women must be protected by the barred windows of the harem from the inordinate desires of men, and in a country where blood-revenge holds sway over the consciousness of law. Thus the theme of constant war against the conventional world order also belongs to the Don Juan type, as Heckel (1915, p. 119) points out; without this struggle the hero would lose all justification for being.

lying character of this wish fantasy by illustrating its exaggeration in another extreme direction. Nevertheless, we can still discern here a fragment of the primitive situation. While he puts *one* fearless hero (namely himself) in place of the many helpers, at the same time he also puts many women in place of the one woman. Here we can see the mechanism by which the trait that really characterizes Don Juan [i.e., the series of women] could arise: through the most extreme alteration, the poet has made a horde of women out of the horde of brothers. The serial form of female sexual objects thus arises from a wish-fulfilling transformation of the harassing clan of brothers.[2]

This explains why the original Don Juan is no darling of women, but rather a seducer, partly by force and partly through cunning, who does not shrink from using

[2] This is the appropriate point to consider the homosexual components that we so often find in the Don Juan type, and that have been observed particularly by Stekel [probably Stekel (1912)]. For a genetic understanding we are indebted to Freud, who recognized as the basic presumption of the heroic orientation that one individual is detached from the homosexual libidinal ties of the mass: thus always the hero alone gets the woman. The arrangement in the clan of brothers entails that the same woman is possessed in common. This motif breaks through at the decisive point in the Don Juan plays, in the relationship of the hero to Leporello. It is remarkable that in his anonymous Don Juan fantasy, Holtei (1834) introduced homosexuality in the strange figure of the sculptor Johannes, who ended up mad. As the tutor of Don Juan, Johannes wished to make his pupil pliable to his own passions, but was scornfully rejected. Heckel (1915, pp. 44-45) finds a personal motive of the artist in a passage from Richard Wagner's posthumous autobiography where the composer declares that Holtei's importunate courtship of his wife was a screen motive for his homosexual inclinations (Wagner, 1911, p. 184).

89

any weapon, so that he really struggles against the women as he does against the men. Here the woman plays anything but the heroic role of helper; on the contrary, she is the real pursuer and avenger of his crime.

Thus the Don Juan fantasy appears to confirm our conjecture that in prehistory the son certainly did not have the help of the mother in vanquishing the father. If we take the conjecture seriously, we must rather admit that the hero also had to struggle against the mother figure—sometimes even until she also perished. The hero's victory was complete when, after eliminating the obstructive primal father, he succeeded in possessing the woman sexually. How hard he had to struggle for this possession is readily evidenced by the many female monsters of myth—from the Babylonian primal mother Tiamat[3] and the Sphinx,[4] to the presumably female vampires

[3] [Heidel (1951) describes the story of Tiamat in his annotated translation of the Babylonian sacred book *Enûma elish* (which dates from approximately 2000 B.C.). Apsu (the freshwater ocean) and Tiamat (the salt-water ocean) were the original divine parents. Distressed at his grandson Ea, Apsu resolved to destroy all his progeny; but Ea used spells and power to slay Apsu while he was asleep, and built a house and shrine for himself upon the slain grandfather.

Tiamat was spared because she was not in sympathy with Apsu's plan. Later, however, her distress was exploited by other gods, so that she was led to avenge Apsu's death. She gave birth to eleven kinds of serpent monsters and dragons, and conferred magical powers upon her new spouse. Ea grew fearful and failed to fight, for Tiamat could not be conquered by magic, but only through physical force. Marduk, his son, agreed to take up the struggle against Tiamat in return for a position of supreme and undisputed authority among the gods. He challenged Tiamat to a duel, at which she cried out in a frenzied fury. When she opened her mouth to devour Marduk, he blew in evil winds so that she could not close her mouth. Then he

of modern Greece; from the overpoweringly dangerous female figures of the legends of Judith[5] and Brünhilde[6] to Isolde, who expresses the archetype of female revenge in Wagner's violent poem:

---

shot an arrow through her open mouth into her distended body; the arrow struck her heart and destroyed her life. Marduk stood on her fallen body, split open her skull with a club, cut her arteries to drain out her blood, and finally cut up the colossal body into two parts. From one part came the sky, and from the other came the earth: thus was the universe created. Tiamat's spouse was then killed in order that man, as a slave for the gods, might be made from his blood.]

[4] [It will be recalled that the Sphinx was a winged figure with a human head and a lion body. By the fourteenth century B.C., the female Sphinx became common in Greece. She terrorized the people by demanding an answer to the riddle: "What has one voice, and yet becomes first four-footed, then two-footed, and lastly three-footed?" Each time the riddle was answered incorrectly, she devoured a man. Oedipus answered the riddle correctly—"Man"—at which the Sphinx killed herself, according to some traditions by throwing herself down upon the rocks. While the etymology of the word is uncertain, some scholars claim that it is related to the Greek verb "to bind" or "to squeeze," which certainly fits with the legend itself and also Rank's interpretation of the mythic female monsters. A scrap of paper in the Rank papers has the note: "The Bad Mother who devours children = Sphinx."]

[5] [The story of Judith is given in the Old Testament Apocrypha book of that name. Judith, a Jewish widow, secured the confidence of Holophernes, an Assyrian general who was besieging the Jewish city of Bethulia on behalf of King Nebuchadnezzar. When alone in his tent with the drunken Holophernes, Judith cut off his head with his own sword, took the severed head in triumph to Bethulia, and thus saved the city.]

[6] [Brünhilde had vowed to marry only a man of exceptional qualities. After passing all the tests, Siegfried wooed and won her, but in fact on behalf of another man. Discovering the treachery, Brünhilde exacted vengeance and death. She appears

As the men are all at peace with Tristan,
Who is there left to strike him down?
(*Tristan und Isolde*, act 1, scene 6)[7]

As to the motive for this negative attitude of the woman, which so strongly contradicts our heroic ideal and its romantic caricature, we can only venture some conjectures based on the few fragments of distorted tradition and analytic insight. Nevertheless, these conjectures are broadly related to psychological truths.

As we learn most vividly from the psychology of the neuroses, the woman continues to have strong libidinal ties to the primal father in spite of all her aversion to his brutal domination. Although she may greatly admire his successor, she is understandably not inclined to lose again to him the freedom that she won through the father's violent death. Actually there is no direct successor to the father from among the horde of brothers, since there are no "heroes." On the contrary, according to Freud's hypothesis,[8] the woman acceded to a dominant position because of the mutual opposition of the "brothers," and she obviously sought to consolidate this position (as by Mother Right, or the Rule of Women).[9] We see traces

in German legends and, with emphasis on her supernatural qualities—as a Valkyrie—in Norse legends. The *Niebelunglied* is the most widely-known source.]

[7] [In Wagner's opera, Tristan had slain Morald, to whom Isolde was bethrothed; Isolde's desire for vengeance was blocked by the gaze of Tristan's eyes. This passage occurs at the end of the boat trip by which Tristan brought her to be the wife of King Mark. Isolde had prepared for Tristan a poison, which was then exchanged for a love potion by her servant.]

[8] [The possessive form and "hypothesis" was added in the manuscript of *B*.]

[9] [See Rank's *Psychology and the Soul* (1930); also Engels (1884) and Bachofen (1967).]

of this situation even today, for example, in the Chinese law that on the death of the father the mother steps out of her silent role into the highest position that a woman can obtain anywhere (Krause, 1922).[10] If the ancestor worship did not pass by her to the son, one could say that she steps into the position of the father himself; but in any case she acquires rights to dispose of the persons and the possessions of the children that are identical to those of the father.

Perhaps we may conjecture here that like the "hero," the "mother" as such did not exist in prehistory; rather, that she appeared at a particular moment when *one* of the many relatively undifferentiated women of the primal horde opposed the brothers and established that she alone should possess the power that had belonged to the father. As a consequence of the primal act, those individual relationships or sentiments that we later find consolidated in the concepts of "father" and "mother" would first crystallize, as it were, out of group psychology. The slain man, whose killing was [later] regretted, furnishes the psychological content of the father concept; the desired and unattainable woman, that of the mother relationship. Probably the woman who progressed psychologically into the mother role also owed this advance to an active sympathy [of the son]. She may well have been a kind of favorite of the slain one, perhaps even a wife. Because she became annoyed at later neglect, her negative feelings toward the ruthless chief of the horde were aroused, so that she protected one of the sons from the persecution of her terrible mate in order to raise him up

[10] [This sentence seems to be based on a newspaper review of the Krause article, probably in the *Neues Wiener Journal*, March 23, 1922, p. 5. A fragment of this article is preserved in the Rank papers.]

as her liberator and avenger. Such an "anaclitic" attachment (in Freud's sense) may perhaps constitute the first nucleus of a mother-son relationship in the sense of individual psychological development as well as that of prehistory. To the protected son, such an attachment may also have suggested that he had a preferred position, so that he was inspired and capable of taking up the struggle against the father and enduring it. Thus while the son acts from clearly libidinal motives, the motives of the woman are strongly ambivalent from the beginning. She always remains libidinally fixated on the primal father, yet on the other hand, she desires the more potent younger [son]. She can submit to this son, however, only if he is successfully identified with the primal father, as in the heroic fantasy. In reality, none of the "brothers" is able to assume the full role of the father at first. Thus although the woman is perhaps no longer altogether attractive sexually, the way is open for her to use the "revolutionary" son as merely an instrument to win the power position of the "mother" for herself as a female revolutionary. As a sign of the paternal power—as the sceptor of the libido, so to speak—the father's phallus appears in the mythic traditions. This is possible because, as the traditions clearly admit, it has been devoured and only survives in a substitute form (see Rank, 1913). The phallus cult that reigned throughout the ancient world is the residue of this female idol, for the woman demanded worship of it in the name of the primal father.

What is the explanation for this special significance of the phallus in the history of religion and cults? We may conjecture that the penis (along with the nourishing warm blood of the slain person, in the vampire beliefs) was the member that the woman herself secured at the terrible totem feast; this she did because of her sexual role. This is suggested by traditions such as the Egyptian one of Isis, who was fertilized by the devoured phallus, even after the death of her consort and by the corresponding custom of the "death marriage" (Naumann, 1921, p. 38; [Schrader, 1904]). Further support comes from the belief in fertilization through the mouth, a belief that is common in fairy tales and that survives today in unconscious fantasies as an infantile wish. From this same root, moreover, also comes the conception of the woman with a penis, which is likewise a typical infantile sexual theory of both primitive peoples and individuals.[11]

In summary,[12] we may say that the characteristic Don Juan fantasy of conquering countless women, which has made the hero into a masculine ideal, is ultimately based on the unattainability of the mother and the compensatory substitute for her. As the fantasy also clearly reveals, this unattainability does not refer to sexual possession, to which there is certainly no barrier in primitive times and character.[13] Rather, it involves the deeply-rooted biological wish for the exclusive and complete possession of the mother, as once experienced in the pleasure of the prenatal situation and forever afterward sought as the highest libidinal satisfaction. Since we have given a comprehensive exposition and proof of this general conception elsewhere (see Rank, 1924b), it is only necessary to note here that from this point of view, both parts of the Don Juan material show an even closer connection. The continually repeated sexual conquest of

[11] [See Rank (1912).]

[12] [These two concluding paragraphs were added in version C.]

[13] [Rank later discusses this assertion in *Psychology and the Soul* (1930, p. 18).]

women remains unsatisfying, for the reason that the infantile tendency to regress to the mother can only be partially fulfilled. In contrast, the death complex, including being devoured again by the corpse-demon, offers the unconscious a much fuller satisfaction of this primal tendency. The devouring animals of the underworld, the grave, and the coffin are clearly unambiguous mother symbols; thus in the punishment that overtakes Don Juan we have not only the expression of the deepest wish-fulfillment—to behold the path of return to the mother— but also a particularly heroic fantasy portrait: the father figure, who otherwise bars access to the mother, now shows the way directly. In the figure of the Stone Guest, who also represents the coffin, appears the mother herself, coming to fetch the son.

Now in order to show that our interpretation of the Don Juan figure as one who has foundered on the mother complex is not just in the service of a predetermined opinion or psychoanalytic theory, we turn to the Don Juan versions themselves. We shall try to show how the poets have handled the role of the woman, and the extent to which they have intuitively recognized the maternal character of this role.

8.

WOMEN IN THE DON JUAN LEGEND

We are about to cite the poets themselves as evidence for our psychoanalytic interpretation, but first it is necessary to give a very general account of the extent to which this is both permissible and fruitful. In the creations of significant artists, psychoanalysis has repeatedly found ample confirmation of its interpretations of psychic events—interpretations that the poet often senses, or feels intuitively, and then puts in artistic form. One of the first problems of applied analysis was to study the deeper conditions of this relationship (Rank, 1907), and since then it has on occasion investigated them in detail. To our surprise, it is evident that poetic fantasy ranges much less freely than we might expect; in creations that are apparently very individualized, poetic fantasy still remains attached to certain unconscious images that could better be called primal images. Thus it is not unusual for later poets to discover the original psychological sense of a motif through elaborating and intensifying it. To some extent, they become thereby unintentional and unwilling precursors of psychoanalysis. The greatest poets, who in the context of their creative work elevate the consistency and astuteness of psychological motivation above all other demands, thus span the latency period (to use a striking phrase of Ferenczi) in humanity's development. Through its overvaluation of the materialistic world-view, such a period of human social development arises between primitive animism and our analytic psychology. This feature of the psychology of the artist is only slightly different from the analytic approach. In his gradual pushing back to the origin of the distorted motif, the artist at the same time presents it in his own original synthetic form; while our psychology, in line with its analytic tendency, is concerned to distinguish between these two factors and to understand them in their mutual interdependence—i.e., to distinguish motif and interpretation with scientific dispassion.

In the concluding chapter we shall have to consider what important psychic and social functions are thus fulfilled by poetic art. At this point we will pursue the real "donjuanesque" character of the hero, namely his relation to women. What interpretations have the poets given to this motif, in the course of the artistic development of the material? Only the hero's wanton playing with the hearts of women is prominent in the *Burlador:*

> There is no talk of love. The driving force is the ambitious striving to seduce or to outdo someone else. He does not know pity for the dishonored ones. . . . The ways in which he tries to accomplish his goal are certainly not very refined. With the Duchess Isabella and Donna Anna de Ulloa, he insinuates his way by night in the disguise of their beloved; with Tisbea and Aminta, the children of nature, he succeeds by the pretense of later marriage. He is truly loved by none of the women. (Heckel, 1915, pp. 9-10)

This original and social Don Juan role, which in the form of its fantasy is closest to the situation of a primal horde of women, has been gradually falsified in a sentimental way by the later poets. To them, such a character evidently seemed too cruel and inhuman, and so they introduced love and even marriage. The first step in this process of "civilizing" the hero was Molière's play (1665) in which Don Juan was changed from a figure of heroic wickedness into a dissolute French nobleman of the times. To be sure, he knows love as little as does the Burlador, but he did abduct Elvira from the convent and marry her. After he left her, she pursues him, and though she is continually deceived, she tries as an earnest admonisher to turn him from the path of depravity:

> Above all, this trait of calm, contented love raises Elvira far above all the other victims of the seducer, even above the Duchess Isabella in the *Burlador*, in whom one would see a precursor of Elvira. (Heckel, 1915, p. 16)

As Heckel further remarked, it is in Molière "that for the first time Don Juan meets such proud, majestic women face-to-face;" the first time, we may emphasize, that one woman is at all elevated out of the series of women who are in his mind equal—or equally inferior.

The next clear step in this development can be seen in the figure created by Mozart's librettist Da Ponte, who:

> made Donna Anna a strong female opposing force, and thus presented Mozart with the opportunity of creating his most complete female figure. . . . In the *Burlador* and also in Gazzaniga (1787), she disappears from the stage forever after her father's death. Mozart was the first to make her into a great personality—the equal of Don Giovanni, although she is as unlike Giovanni as is possible. She is the true champion and avengeress of the violated sense of honor and *love for the murdered father; to her, sensual passion is entirely alien*. . . . (Heckel, pp. 22, 24-25 [Rank's emphasis])

99

In the service of a tightly constructed plot, later versions gradually satisfied themselves with fewer and fewer loves. Grabbe (1829) even had a single one, while Tolstoi (1860) only presented the relationship with Donna Anna, and Rittner (1909) even personified the most faithful husband in his adversary Leporello.[1]

Thus we see that the original Don Juan type, in the course of its poetic development, moves from the ruthless seducer of women to a romantic and finally a civilized lover, and ends at a point where the heroic lie is given up in favor of a romantic explanation. In the course of this process, however, the character of the real Don Juan is also effaced. As Lenau's (1851) version best shows, the hero himself is:

> no longer a genial offender, but rather one who struggles and fights for his ideal; no longer one who in disillusion and boredom has given up striving for the highest goal, but rather one who seeks it all his life. (Heckel, p. 82)

"My Don Juan," Lenau himself said, "could not be a hot-blooded man eternally chasing after women. It is his yearning to find a woman who is the incarnation of womanhood, and through whom he could enjoy all the women of the world, although he cannot possess them individually."

When the poets, in the original situation of the serial form [of seduced women], introduced the mother figure into the material out of the psychological need for denial, they destroyed the hero characterologically; often

---

[1] [As the secretary to the Baron (Don Juan), Leporello refuses to let his wife, whom he loves tenderly, have any contact with the seducer, and even goes so far as to kill Don Juan to prevent it.]

100

they even had him destroyed physically by the single beloved woman. The many later versions in which Don
Juan meets death at the hand of an abandoned beloved
woman also belong here. Such an end is as unsuited to
his character as could be, but it repeats an important
motif of our reconstructed prehistory: namely that the
jealousy of the *individual* woman makes impossible [any
simple] repetition of the polygamous original type. We
can easily recognize the mother figure who replaces the
inhibiting father in the admonishing role of Donna Elvira, who as champion of the violated moral law walks
in the footsteps of the mother who avenges the murder
of the father. In the figure of Donna Anna a fragment of
the original motivation is still clear. This fragment is the
ambivalent attitude of the daughter to the murdered
primal father, so that she partly welcomes the murderer
as a liberator and a new beloved, and partly scorns and
persecutes him as a weaker substitute for the lost primal
object. In the prehistorical sense, the daughter becomes
not only the bad mother, but also the faithless mother—
a characteristic that perhaps may have been passed on to
the Don Juan type itself. Traces of this untrue mother
are found in the later versions, as in Holtei (1834) and
Byron (1819-24), who gave the hero a fickle mother, or
in Pushkin (1830), where Laura is as faithless and wanton as the hero himself.

The whole primal historical role of the bad mother
and the hero who is deceived by her appears in one of
the newest, but also most profound, Don Juan versions,
Bernard Shaw's "Man and Superman" (1903). In the
disguise of an anti-romantic play turned into caricature,
this role reaches its final flowering. The hero, an English
gentleman and theoretical revolutionary, struggles with
all the means of modern ideas and technology against a

101

fate which he cannot avert—to be married against his will to Donna Anna. In the end, his philosophy, which is based on the evil and danger of woman, cannot protect him from this earthly hell—in comparison with which the real hell of the ancient Don Juan, which he sees in a dream, is more acceptable than even a sojourn in heaven. He knows that woman aspires to domination over man and achieves it, and he is clear that she uses man only as the instrument of her natural purposes. He outdoes himself in the multitude of his really strange and primitive comparisons of woman: with a spider, who entices man into a web in order to suck out his blood; with a boa constrictor, who inextricably embraces him; and with a wild beast, who swallows him up as a defenseless prey.

Perhaps one will not think it justified to draw conclusions of so far-reaching a kind from such indications of poetry that was apparently intended for wholly different purposes. Still one must consider that we are concerned with the ramifications of overlapping lines of development. While we are inclined to trace these back to the operation of definite, far-reaching mental principles, it would lead us too far away from the scope of the present study to discuss and establish these processes fully. Our interest now lies more in another direction: namely to pursue the dynamic processes that run parallel to the poetic preservation and progressive clarification of the motif. These processes furnish the actual instinctual force for artistic production, and their affective consequence constitutes one of the most important social functions of the poetic art.

9.

THE LEGEND OVER TIME

THE DEVIL: *I see that you read
too much what has been written
about you!*

Rostand[1]

HAVING traced the psychological motives of the
original Don Juan figure from its primal historical roots
up through its most recent poetic branches, our remaining task is to pursue the individual artistic modifications
of the material from its medieval origin in the Christian
conception of sin.

The oldest appearance of Don Juan in world literature
is a Spanish comedy, now apparently lost, that appeared
at about the end of the sixteenth century. The *Burlador*
is a slightly altered form of this play. For a very long
time this work was attributed to the monk Fray Gabriel
Téllez, a prolific dramatist who is known by the name
Tirso de Molina. More recently, this authorship has been
disputed in favor of the great Calderón.[2] The question

---

[1] [From Rostand's *La dernière nuit de Don Juan* (1921), second part. Don Juan has just described his courage and indif-
ference to laws and customs. The devil replies, "Je crois que
tu lis trop, ce qu'on écrit sur toi!"]

[2] [The *Burlador* had been generally attributed to Tirso until
this authorship was challenged by Farinelli (1896) and some
other scholars. In his comprehensive study of the origins of the
play, Wade (1969) argues that Tirso was beyond doubt the
author. He apparently wrote two slightly different versions:

103

of authorship is not important for us, for in any case we do not know much about the personality of the first poet and creator of Don Juan other than the most general knowledge drawn from his times and his works.[3] From these scanty data one can only surmise what may have drawn the rather unknown author to the traditional material of the Stone Guest. This figure had already appeared in the *Infamador*, by Juan de la Cuerva, which was produced in Seville in 1581, and in the Leontine plays,[4] in which the gruesome elements were depicted more flagrantly. In these plays the hero was presented as the usual ruthless, vicious sort, and death simply came to avenge his crimes. In the *Burlador*, however, the offense

---

the *Burlador* and *¿Tan largo me lo fiáis?* The latter was rediscovered in 1878; for some time its authorship was uncertain and so it may be the "oldest presentation" to which Rank refers.]

[3] [If Tirso was indeed the author, then recent scholarship has established many more important details about his personality and his times (see Wade, 1969; Winter, 1973, Chapter 6). Tirso was probably born in 1584, and was probably the illegitimate and unrecognized son of the Duke of Osuna, Don Juan Téllez Girón. He had a sister who was both as clever and as unhappy as he was. He often used his plays to give advice to those in positions of power, to serve as propaganda, and to attack important and prominent people. Perhaps for these reasons, he was declared "a danger to public morals" in 1625, and was forbidden to write further plays. He probably wrote the *Burlador* in 1616, while spending time in Seville, prior to his departure for the New World on a mission for his order, the Mercedarians. The theme of the powerful, deceiving, and exploiting woman is quite prominent in his other plays. Every one of these details is quite consistent with Rank's analysis of the artist, in this book generally and in the next chapter specifically.]

[4] [Weinstein (1959, pp. 10-11) discusses the extent of overlap of these plays with the Don Juan legend.]

to the exalted person is increased; and the punishment is conceived as the instrument of eternal heavenly justice. One could say that the author of the *Burlador*, living in orthodox times, was motivated by this ethical-religious impulse to rework the traditional material of avenging death. Yet such a motive is both too general and too incomplete to be taken as the basis for an analysis of a poetic individual. Fortunately there is a second and more interesting question that can help us in this difficulty: How was the poet inclined to arrive at the figure of Don Juan and the connection with the legend of avenging death?

Again, this question can be answered only on the basis of an intimate knowledge of the personality of the first poet—knowledge that is unavailable to us. We believe, however, that the solution has rather easily fallen into our lap already, as an unexpected further yield from our analysis of the motif [of avenging death]. It is only a matter of applying to the whole of the poem the "principle of elucidation" of poetic form which we established in the pursuit of a single motif. The primal crime that we find embodied in the fantasy portrait of the Don Juan figure has yielded to our analytic understanding of the primal human anxiety about avenging death. In other words, the first Don Juan poet (whether or not he might have been a historical personality) has given us the psychological meaning of the vengeance of death, and has embodied this meaning in a dramatic figure that is both eternal, and yet, as we have seen, capable of metamorphosis. Because of a strong personal and social[5] sense of guilt acting from within, he has fantasized, in addition to the traditional punishment, the crime that psycho-

---

[5] [*Säkularen*]

logically corresponds to it.[6] Indeed, from the primal situation itself, we have even succeeded in freely deducing the form of Oedipal orientation[7] that characterizes Don Juan exactly: the most extreme mocking of the dead with an invitation to the banquet, as well as the serial form of sexual objects.

Thus the *Burlador* presents a complete reworking of the original material in the direction of the most extreme fantasy wish. He is, as it were, the heroic figure, standing at the beginning of the "poetic" accounts of individual psychology.[8] The later poems, in contrast, appear to correspond to the subsequent legendary elaboration in different ways—not only in the breakthrough of the originally repressed elements on the one hand, and in the artistic interpretation of these elements on the other, but more importantly in a progressive *devaluation*[9] *of the material* that corresponds to *the conquering of the guilt feelings*, the *denial* of which represents the original Don Juan type.

For the Burlador is precisely the "blasphemer" who scoffs at conscience as it is represented in the comical figure of his servant, and whose tendency to devalue all social and spiritual values that are opposed to himself even reaches to a euphemistic denial of death, with which

[6] [I take Rank's point here to be that the first poet was aware of the legends of punishment by avenging death, and that his inner sense of guilt led him to construct, in fantasy, a crime—serial seduction of women—that would be appropriate to or "deserve" such a punishment.]

[7] [Rank changed "Oedipal crime" to "orientation" in the proofs of *B*.]

[8] ["Individual psychology," in the sense of the evolution from "group psychology," as it existed in the primal horde. See Freud's use (1921, pp. 135-36).]

[9] [*Entwertung*]

he tries to pledge a hearty brotherhood.[10] Consequently, the psychological sense of this action would be to show that although man has the ability to endure heroically all other powers, he founders on the inner inhibitions that are manifested in his ego ideal, his conscience, his guilt feelings, and his anxiety about retribution. We have noted the ways in which the further development of the material clarifies this punishment tendency by means of the accumulation of offenses, "and in fact almost all Don Juans in the first half of the nineteenth century . . . are little more than common criminals" (Heckel, 1915, p. 68). Certainly connected with this development is the fact that the intrinsically lustful fantasy wish of unrestrained erotic impulse steadily gives up its primitive qualities and lack of restraint. The development finally leads to a characterological death and thus extinction of the original type, which threatens to founder on a sense of guilt that has become overpowering, quite in the way that neurotics founder on guilt feelings. At such a point only the poet's art of interpretation helps, by unburdening the character through a process of devaluation of the guilt feelings and by making possible a pretended existence for a time.

After all that we have learned about the psychological conditions of dramatic production, we are not surprised if the process of artistic elucidation of a theme often recalls the analytic interpretation. The artistic-synthetic presentation of the Don Juan material culminates in Mozart's immortal masterpiece. Here the sense of guilt breaks through so powerfully that it leads on the one

[10] [*Mit dem er lustige Bruderschaft zu trinken versucht.* The German phrase also means the ritual in which acquaintances switch from the formal second-person pronoun (*"Sie"*) to the intimate pronoun (*"du"*).]

hand to its clearest manifestation in the father complex (the Commander), and on the other hand to the complete inhibition of the libido (which was originally unrestrained) for the forbidden maternal object. The result of this second effect is that the whole series of women remains unattainable for the hero.

The poetic shaping of the material actually shows us that when it reaches the point of elucidating the unconscious psychic content, it is no longer capable of any further development in that direction. Thus the true *psychological interpretation* of the Don Juan figure begins at that point. Heckel dates this beginning from E. T. A. Hoffman (1813) in Germany, and in France, under the influence of Hoffman, from Alfred de Musset (1832). At the end of the nineteenth century it culminated in the prevailing view "that sees in Don Juan no longer the great criminal, but rather a fighting and struggling *human being* whose faithlessness arises from his quest for the ideal woman and his overpowering impulse life" (Heckel, 1915, pp. 64-65 [Rank's emphasis]). Heckel called this view "the first psychological explanation of the Don Juan problem," because for the first time it asked and tried to answer the question, *"How did Don Juan become what he is?"* (p. 70). One could almost term the answers to the question psychoanalytic, in that they reduce the heroic lie to purely human features, though to be sure in the light of a romantic explanation. Thus the psychological interpretations of the nineteenth century destroyed the real character of the hero, and this result surely explains the fact that Hoffman's analysis of Don Juan aroused so much strong opposition, even in his devoted biographer Ellinger (1912).

It is interesting, then, to pursue the ways in which the poetic attempt to explain the Don Juan character really corresponds to the analytic process of interpretation, with the one difference that poetic explanations seek to use the results of interpretation for the presentation of a new motif. In this way we learn how the poets advance the development of a character that is already in literature and we gain the impression that they obviously succeed at such a challenge by the same technique that the first Don Juan poet adopted, i.e., that they try to derive the psychological motivation out of their own unconscious. Therefore, we shall not be surprised to find that here and there scattered parts of the original motive reemerge in these widely proliferating fantasies about Don Juan. If one were to pursue the process in detail, one could almost formulate sets of motives designated by the terms "anamnestic,"[11] "etiological," and "symptomatological," according to the respective author's interest in childhood memoirs, effects of environment, or maladjustments resulting from it.[12] To the first set belongs, for example, the detailed descriptive record of Don Juan's childhood in the eleven-volume novel by Félicien Mallefille (1852). In this account, the hero was endowed in childhood with abundant fantasy and a precocious love life, which made love seem unsatisfying to him at an early age. As a prototype of the etiological motivation, one would cite the poem of Byron (1819-24), who had the hero grow up under the influence of an overly affectionate mother and an unfaithful, plainly "donjuanesque" father, about whose escapades the mother kept a "catalogue." The identification with the father then finds poetic expression in the first romantic adventure of the sexually unenlightened hero with an obviously unfaithful "mother figure." It con-

[11] ["Anamnestic" refers to the recollection of relevant events that occur prior to the onset of an illness or disorder.]

[12] [The last clause is added in version G.]

109

tinues in the heroically-tinged rescue of the principal character by a tender loving woman.[13] In his presentation of another typical Oedipal destiny, Julius Hart (1881) had the hero deceived and betrayed in his first pure love. Holtei (1834) pushed this deception, with all of its analytic consequences, back to the first deception in love by the mother. He made the hero the fruit of his mother's fall from virtue—a fact that is known to him and that serves as the motivation of his character ("Surely you would not demand that I should be one of the elect, since you have told me that I am your bastard son?").

If we see the Oedipal motive emerging in the etiology, then logically the symptomatology should show the same characteristics. What does a Don Juan, who has developed in this way, do then? In his youthful drama *Les adieux de Don Juan* [Don Juan's farewell] (1844), Count Gobineau borrowed from Byron the overly affectionate mother who warps her son. As an analytic consequence, the first passion of elementary sensuality was kindled with Donna Claudia, the beautiful wife of Don Sancho, who was the hero's brother and who himself had meagre natural endowments. Because of this tragic love adventure, Don Juan was compelled to leave the house of his parents and satisfy his desires for the pleasures of love elsewhere. We find the same primal heroic motif—the hero in a conflict for the wives of his brothers—earlier in Dumas; Alfred Friedmann later made it the basis of his play, *Don Juans letztes Abenteuer* [Don Juan's last adventure] (1881). This motif, which derives from the community of brothers and which in Mozart still finds an echo in the common possession of

[13] It is noteworthy that ancient primitive elements are embedded in this romantic, heroic idyll. Thus the real theme of the famous second canto about the storm at sea is cannibalism.

the same woman by master and servant (Amphitryon motif), also appears in the description of the aged Don Juan by the Swedish dramatist Almqvist (1854). Here the dependence on the primal form of the motif is clearer: Ramido, the young son of Don Juan, was denied the good fortune of love because each of the four young girls who attracted his heart turned out to be the daughter of Don Juan. Ramido fled from the beloved sisters in bitter disillusionment. The tragedy by Paul Heyse, *Don Juans Ende* [Don Juan's end] (1883), can be understood in the same sense of primal restitution; complete with all of the requirements of a romantic drama of destiny, the old Don Juan appeared as a competitor with his own son for love.

It seems that as the subject matter has grown older, so also has the depiction of the aging Don Juan grown in popularity among the poets. Such descriptions make it clear that an impulse toward devaluation is a consequence of the psychological problem of the aging Don Juan, and this devaluation increasingly wins the upper hand. The devaluation involves not only the mere humanizing of the hero, but rather reaches a point of involuntary ridicule that finally falls into conscious caricature.

In terms of their characteristics, all of these versions belong to the nineteenth and twentieth centuries, according to Heckel's description (1915, pp. 142ff.). "A naive age, less inclined to psychological brooding, never came to the point of raising the question common to all of these plays: What will become of Don Juan when he grows old?" For the first time, Theophile Gautier conjured out of the grave the ghost of the aged Don Juan in his *Comédie de la Mort* [Comedy of death] (1838). With false hair, false teeth, and an enfeebled body, the mouldering roué laments his youth that was dissipated

111

in debauchery. Not much different is the end of the *Don Juan* of the Portuguese writer Guerra Junqueiro (1874). *Don Juan Barbon*, a one-act play by Gustave Levavasseur (1848), seems almost farcical. Confined to bed by gout and arthritis, the one-time lover of women has to experience his pupil Don Sancho cheating him out of his wife and seducing his daughter—in strict accordance with the talion law. In defending the honor of his house with his sword, Don Juan falls at the hand of his superior opponent. Jules Viard (1853) also gives the aged seducer the prize for absurdity. The only love that is still available to him is the kind that is to be had for money, and he fails miserably in an attempt to seduce the fiancée of his son. His own son gives him a beating, and in the end he only succeeds in being shut out of his house by his wife and son.

Here we see the theme of the aging Don Juan brought down to his fatherhood and his disturbed relationship to his children. Although these features are distorted into ridicule by the bourgeois mind, they are not a departure from the deeper psychological motivation; for the last ramification of the tragic guilt feelings is manifest in them in the form of the retaliatory revenge of the second generation. As the problems of guilt and punishment are cheapened and made superficial—in Lavedan (1902)[14] the hero perishes in a paralysis—it is unmistakably clear that a psychological presentation of these problems has reached the limit of presentation. When the hero goes beyond that limit, he has taken the feared step from the

---

[14] *Le marquis de Priola*. [The marquis of Priola]. It is characteristic that the French push the hero down to the level of ordinary humanity, while in moralistic England, even Byron's *Don Juan* is rejected; and that neither before nor since would the tabooed material be treated in an undistorted way.

noble to the ridiculous. If it were necessary to cite examples, one could list here all of the very many bad Don Juan versions; for no poet has succeeded in mastering the material in a fully artistic way.

At this point it is interesting to study the origin of another development that culminates in the *conscious* devaluation and ironic treatment of the hero, a theme that really shifts the comic-criticizing role of the servant back to the master himself. In the German popular theatre of the eighteenth century, of which only one play has come down to us,[15] the predominant element was already a rather rough and vulgar comedy, in comparison to which the serious scenes were insignificant; the puppet plays can also be mentioned as a similar example. The main content of these plays is the coarse jokes of Hanswurst or Kasperl, who play the role of Don Juan's servant. This certainly involves a primitive thematic counterpoise to the terrible murder and punishment scenes that, in contrast, appear at their most extreme height in the eighteenth-century horror plays. "Regularly until 1772 in Vienna, during the week following the Festival of All Souls, there played *Don Juan oder das Steinere Gastmahl* [Don Juan or the Stone Guest], of which we know nothing more" (Heckel, 1915, p. 18); and even in present-day Spain, Zorrilla's famous play *Don Juan Tenorio* (1844) is produced in all of the theatres of

[15] *Donn Joann, ein Schauspill in 4 Aufzigen*, by Herr appen Beter Metastasio, which has come down to us through a transcript by Franz Kastner in 1811. See Werner (1891), as cited in Heckel (1915, p. 18). [This play was performed by the men who worked in the transport system on the river Salzach and lived in the town of Laufen. During the winter months, they organized travelling theatrical troupes to earn money. Singer (1965, p. 42) says that the attribution to Metastasio is wrong.]

the country every year during the fortnight after November 1, just as Raupach's play *Der Müller und sein Kind* [The miller and his child] is performed in Austria.[16]

> The portrayal of the banquet that the Commander gives for Don Juan in the mausoleum of the Tenorio family, in which the table is decorated with serpents, bones, and fire, and ashes and fire are set out as food and drink, is somewhat unpleasant to our feelings; still less can one reconcile oneself to the ghosts and skeletons of Don Juan's victims who inhabit the cemetery in this scene, and in the end fall upon him. (Heckel, 1915, p. 58)

Corresponding to this oppressive sense of guilt, the hero is painted in the darkest of colors. He is a criminal, absolutely unrestrained by any thoughts of conscience, who would fashion an *eating utensil* out of the *bones* of those who perished through his fault.[17] If we compare the showy cemetery ghost in Raupach with this very primitive element, then we can estimate both the quite terrible growth of the sense of guilt and also the devaluation that is necessary to its relief.

In this connection there emerges a new motif, perhaps original, but in any case one that has been altered in a sentimental direction. We can trace it back to the earliest literary development. In addition to the ghosts of the slain men, whose original forms represent conscience in the sense of the father complex (the Commander), there

[16] [*Bei uns*]

[17] [When his courage is challenged, Don Juan says of the corpses, "I am man enough to make dishes of their skulls." Zorilla, *Don Juan Tenorio*, part 2, act 1, scene 6.]

also appear the ghosts of his female victims who, quite in the sense of our interpretation, easily substitute for the pursuing and avenging horde of men. This feminization of conscience often goes along with the comical and self-ironical elements, as for example in Lenau's otherwise thoroughly serious poem. Under the leadership of Don Pedro, many of the abandoned women, even with their children, intrude upon the seducer in order to take revenge upon him. Similarly, in Baudelaire's poem *Don Juan aux enfers* [Don Juan in hell] (1846), there appear the accusing voices of his victims, dressed in tattered clothes, baring their flabby breasts to him. The aged father, trembling, shows the dead to the wicked son who had scoffed at his grey hair. Sganarelle laughingly demands his wages. Also in Rittner's drama (1909), the conscience of the hero betrays him to the defrauded servant, by whom he is cut down without offering resistance. Drawn by a secret power, as if in a dream, his victims then assemble around his body. His brother, a sober professor, has the room emptied of the women. Only one—his last love, and the wife of Leporello—stays on and kisses the dead hero on the lips, so that while both rejoicing and at the same time startled, she calls out, "He has returned my kiss!"

In the marionette theatre versions, the burlesque element is particularly important in Friedmann's drama (1881), where the author:

> obviously in order to prove the identity of his hero with the Don Juan of legend, has him and Leporello discuss the adventures he had had in the well-known Don Juan plays (Mozart, Zorilla, Grabbe). Leporello reflects: "What has become of the Annas and the El-

viras now? The Zerlinas and Masettos? The commander and all the marionettes that we once had dancing on the strings of our passion in the puppet theatre that we called our youth?" And Don Juan replies mournfully: "Fathers of families, Leporello. Fat mothers, Leporello. Grandmothers who rock their grandchildren on their trembling knees;—Guests for the society of worms who mutually invite each other to a feast; or, if they were thin and haggard, to herring-banquets of worms after their frantic carnival under the land of the moles." (Heckel, 1915, pp. 132-33)

In the *Don Juan* of Bernhardi (1903), the hero himself appears in an even more thorough devaluation, as the actor of his own role just before he returns to his home at the end of the play.

It is the annual fair, and a "brand-new play" called *Don Juan's Adventure* is to be given by one of the troupes that has appeared. However, when the heroine was supposed to appear, her partner waits for her and tries to help matters with some very inept extemporizing—in vain—and the audience begins to be restless. Finally the director appears and makes the surprising announcement that the original of the hero, unrecognized, has been at the performance, has won the affection of the actress, and has eloped with her. Relying on Don Juan's inconstancy, the director boldly invites the public to a repeat performance of the comedy, "First in order to become acquainted with the actress, who now appears in a more interesting light through her relationship to the amorous knight Don Juan, and also to be present at the abduction of Esmeralda from the theatre." (Heckel, 1915, p. 103)

Both of these last two versions make use of Don Juan's literary existence: his adventures take place only within the well-known plays, certainly for the sensationalism of the audience. Such an existence shows the tendency to devaluation in the service of the psychological interpretation, a tendency that recognizes the lying fantasy wish behind the heroic Don Juan character. The most recent Don Juan work, Edmund Rostand's posthumous dramatic poem *La dernière nuit de Don Juan* [The last night of Don Juan] (1921), which was first published in Paris in 1921 and was produced in the spring of 1922 at the Théâtre Porte-Saint-Martin, shows a devaluation that is consciously even more thorough. The famous Thousand and Three appear as nothing but shadows of the underworld, brought up by Satan, who trouble the conscience of the worldly Don Juan. With almost Shavian irony, his punishment is that he does not end up in the great hell, but rather in a little hell of painted canvas in the marionette theatre. As a puppet, he has to act out eternal adulteries, while his heroic pride demands the approaching hellfire of literature. After all he is a Don Juan who is certainly aware of his fame and who knows the respect he owes to his evil fame and his literary tradition. He is intentionally drawn by the poet in a rather unreal way, as his own successor or shadow, as it were. The prologue of the play returns to the scene that otherwise serves to end Don Juan tragedies—the Commander descends into hell, and Don Juan follows him pensively, at each step murmuring the name of another woman. The stone avenger is filled with admiration at such magnanimity—just as in the Shavian dream hell—and wants to pardon him. However, a gigantic hand rises out of the background and points its finger at the condemned one.

It is Satan, and Don Juan mockingly asks him for another interval of ten years to continue his dissolute life.[18]
The play itself is set in Venice at the end of this interval.
Set free from the vengeance of hell, the hero has lived
riotously. A puppet artist passes by and performs an unusual comedy with his fingers: Punchinello parodies the
famous seducer Don Juan, who then jokes with the pup-
pets and teaches them his principle of scorning the devil
himself. The puppet wagers that he cannot do it any
more, and Don Juan shakes the wooden hand in agreement on the wager. Then the puppeteer reveals himself
as the devil come to claim his victim, but Don Juan invites him to a sumptuous meal and in the course of the
conversation proudly shows him his list. Satan tears it
into pieces, which are then transformed into a flotilla of
dusky gondolas as they fall into the lagoon. In a vast
procession, the shadows of the Thousand and Three
abandoned victims arise from the flotilla and surround
him more and more closely. The devil, who increasingly
takes over the role of Don Juan's own conscience, puts
him to a test. This test consists of recognizing the soul
of a particular woman from a few whispered words, for
Don Juan denied that he only recognized the woman's
body. And now begins a long dialogue of pathetic di-
mensions between the defendant, whose arrogant pride
is shaken, and the shadows, who slowly and relentlessly
destroy his illusions, one after the other. He has known
only masks; always they have lied to him, and he himself
wanted those lies, for the woman appears to the man as he
wishes her to be. The avenging women reveal to him
how pitiable his imagined seduction technique had been:
the women conquered him, and if he left them, it was

[18] The forgivingness of the Commander is already found in
Zorilla, and certainly not in an ironic sense.

because the unadmitted fear of having to remain with one of them drove him to it. Finally, a more distinct white shadow emerges. In her eyes are tears of sympathy that pour out the torment of the man who is never satisfied and who is always seeking anew a woman. This white shadow, a symbol of the ideal and an emanation from all the other shadows, was in each of them and Don Juan could easily have found it with a little love. However, he had let all these opportunities pass and now suffers from his sterility.

In a psychological way, this conscious devaluation of the Don Juan type pulls apart the last shreds of his heroic character bit by bit, and forces the bold conquering hero to capitulate before a host of sentimental memories of love that distress his conscience. This is truly Don Juan's last night, his real literary end![19]

[19] [Rank changed "his real psychological end" to the present wording in correcting the proofs of *B*. In the Rank papers, there is a scrap of paper with the following words: "Rostand—*fingers*! Masturbation fantasy! Hand out of the *grave*!" and another: "Hand reaches toward him out of the grave!"]

10.

THE PSYCHOLOGY OF THE POET

We have followed in rough outline the process of poetic shaping and modification of the subject matter. This process shows the double function and effect of the poetic art. Up to a certain point, the primal motives underlying the poetic fantasy construction are expressed. As the guilt feelings increase and become intolerable, this expression gradually gives way to a devaluation of the tragic subject matter. The devaluation corresponds to the mastery of the problem of guilt. Beyond a certain definite point, however, the presentation of the unconscious motive becomes repellent through its coarseness just as it becomes ineffectual and inartistic through psychological interpretation. In both extremes, poetic art approaches a limit. Beyond this limit is the domain of psychoanalysis, which is able to judge and criticize on an intellectual basis rather than devaluing on affective grounds. The artistic function of poetic art corresponds to this catharsis: presenting in the content of poetry the primitive complexes of mankind, in their actual state of repression at any particular time. As is shown especially in the development of tragic subject matter, this repression occurs when the primitive fantasy wishes are bound up with a continually increasing sense of guilt. One of the foremost functions of the poetic art is to relieve these guilt feelings that have accumulated in the course of mankind's repressions. In the first instance, this takes place through the artistic presentation itself, but later it is brought about by the psychological interpretation of

120

the character, and finally by the increasingly conscious devaluation. In the course of this process, the poet has set himself up as an analytical agency of conscience for humanity, which fully accords with the individual goals and purposes of poetry in the service of the ego ideal. Now in the poet we see a very special function, since the ego ideal appears as the critical agency in its formation of the ideal itself, so that it is continually valuing and devaluing itself.

Therefore we see that the poet embodies the double function of the ego ideal. Seen from the outside, the poet creates a new personal ideal for the masses, a creation to which he was driven by his inner conflicts arising from the formation of his own ideal. Dissatisfied with the ideal of the group,[1] he forms his own individual ideal in order to proffer it to the group, without whose recognition his creation remains very unsatisfactory. The impetus to his formation of an individual ideal obviously comes from a very strong narcissism, which prevents him from accepting the common ideal and makes it necessary for him to create an individual one. Seen from the inside, the pressure that the poet feels to solicit recognition of his new ideal from the group reveals that he created it not only to satisfy his own narcissism, but also to replace the old common ideal with a new one. In a psychological sense the poet thereby repeats the primal crime, for the new ideal which he has created is his own —it is himself in identification with the primal father. With unrelenting acuteness, Shaw expressed this psychological state of affairs in his Don Juan play. He characterized the artist as an anti-social, inconsiderate, cruel and primitive man who consciously placed himself outside society, proclaimed the freedom of his desire, and

[1] [*Das Ideal der Masse*]

121

ruptured all family and connubial life. At this point it becomes very clear *that characterologically the poet type converges with the "hero" type*—the type that in its most extreme characteristics is truly shown in the Don Juan figure. Perhaps these psychological facts explain why all the poets necessarily failed in the presentation of this all too unadorned self-portrait; why on the one hand they flattered it, and on the other hand they tried to devalue it. It was too true to life, and it was the ego ideal, strengthened by the guilt feeling, that gradually prohibited the presentation of this original type in order to make a romantic ideal figure out of it. Only in this deeper sense can one agree with Plato, who wanted to banish the poet from his ideal state as a liar (and only permit the physician to lie in order to comfort others),[2] because the poet is distinguished from the hero by a socially important characteristic. The poet makes the falsification of presentation his own inherent, special right, thereby advancing the claim that he has replaced the heroic fantasy construction with a moral form of the ideal. The tragedy of every great poetic personality is that when this aim succeeds, it must finally lead to disappointment instead of satisfaction, just as the primal deed does. The reason is that as his personal ideal is generally recognized and appreciated, it becomes established as another group ideal, the very thing that he wishes to shun. He uses recognition only as evidence of his exoneration, as it were. It is evidence that he is not the only person with the inclination toward the primal deed, although he alone carried it out and repeats it by creating a new ideal—his own. Yet he is disturbed by the general popularizing of this ideal that necessarily goes along with recognition, for it

[2] [*The Republic*, sections 376-92 and 595-607. The phrase in parentheses was added by Rank in the proofs of *B.*]

demonstrates to him that with his personal creation he has accomplished nothing original, that on the contrary he can only repeat the original ideal which has been denied. In the same way, still another expectation of the poet is necessarily disappointed. The strong primary narcissism that we have postulated makes him less inclined toward object love and places him in the more feminine situation of being loved. He transfers a great part of this primary narcissism secondarily on to his work, which he loves, values, and admires as an immortal part of his ego.[3] Yet when he evokes the same orientation in the masses, then the primary libidinal gain—aspiring to be loved oneself—escapes him.

It would be very instructive to pursue these two phases of the poetic orientation in detail with several poets, but we must here be content with the general point that whenever we find distinct periods in the work of a poet,[4] such a process of devaluation of the poet's previous ego ideal formation is at work. (The poet becomes more critical, more conscious, more pessimistic, etc.) We certainly do not need to go even that far; for the fact that the poet generally keeps producing, even must produce, shows us the process of devaluation of the most recent ideal formation and a renewed attempt at a fresh ideal formation—really all in a constant flow. From another perspective, a psychoanalytic glance at the developmental history of poetry is sufficient to show us that, on the whole, the same process runs its course and continually recurs. According to Freud, the first epic tale was a mythic-ideal formation, as also were many of the early

[3] [This phrase suggests the transition to Rank's later vocabulary, in which "ego ideal" (never "superego") was replaced by "immortal soul" or "immortal self."]

[4] Cf. Rank (1912), especially the footnote on page 97.

works of the poetic *Sturm und Drang* period. Soon, however, the critical voice of the ego ideal comes into play, supporting the punishment tendency. Thus the consciousness of guilt mounts, rising to a peak at an end point of our western literary development in Ibsen's conscious recognition:[5]

> *To live* is—a war with trolls
> in the vaults of heart and mind.
> *To write poetry—that is to hold
> judgment day on one's self.*

Naturally, we do not know much about the creator of the Don Juan figure, nor which personal motives gave rise to that magnificent creation of fantasy. We do, however, know a biographical fact about Mozart—the artist who endowed this creation with its immortal form—that clearly illuminates his attitude toward the whole subject

[5] ["Et Vers" (A verse) in Henrik Ibsen, *Samlede Værker,* vol. 4, p. 433 (Copenhagen: Gyldendalske Boghandels Forlag, 1899). The present version has been translated directly from the Norwegian. The emphases are Rank's. The German version used by Rank is as follows:

> *Leben* heisst—dunkler Gewalten
> Spuk bekämpfen in sich,
> *Dichten*—Gerichstag halten
> Über sein eigenes Ich.

Source: *Henrik Ibsens Sämtliche Werke,* vol. 1, p. 167 (Ed. G. Brandes, J. Elias, and P. Schleuther), 1903.
The two preceding paragraphs of the text, along with the verse from Ibsen, appear in almost exactly this form as the conclusion of Rank's Foreword to the fourth, expanded edition of *Der Künstler* (Rank's first publication, 1907), which was published in 1925. Rank dated that Foreword "Vienna, Easter, 1924," seven days before his first departure for America and the formal beginning of the break with Freud.]

of Don Juan, as well as the essence of artistic production itself. Once again, it was not the erotic motive that inspired the great composer, but rather a tragic motive, the important effect of which Freud has already made clear in the life of another great artist.[6] The fact is that just as Mozart had begun to occupy himself with the material that his librettist Da Ponte had submitted, *his father died* and a few months later his best friend Barisani also died.[7] The biographers themselves emphasize that the artist sought an opportunity to set free his distressed heart, and the great intensity with which he plunged into the work is reported everywhere. The clearest evidence of the artistic "possession" that his associates observed in him is that he wrote down the overture in a single night. According to our psychoanalytic experience, the death of the father arouses deeply ambivalent stirrings of affect, especially in the creating artist. These affective stirrings explain the artistic penetration and mastery of the subject matter, an attainment that is made possible only on the basis of a far-reaching identification [with the father]. Of all the authors who attempted this mastery, only Mozart succeeded.[8]

[6] [Rank cites no specific work of Freud's, but probably refers to *Leonardo da Vinci and a Memory of his Childhood* (1910a).]

[7] Da Ponte showed the *Don Giovanni* material to the composer in the spring of 1787, after the return journey from Prague to Vienna. Mozart himself had a great share in the actual dramatic form of the opera. His father died on May 28, 1787; his friend died on September 3; and the first performance of the opera took place on October 29. The ink on the musical score of the overture was still wet, with grains of blotting sand clinging to it, when the musicians received it.

[8] A hundred years ago, Stendhal (1814), one of the most subtle connoisseurs of Mozart, pointed to the melancholy at the root of his "cheerful" art. Now the most recent Mozart biog-

125

Because of our limited psychological understanding of musical forms of expression, we can only surmise what share the particular art form of music may have had in this accomplishment, along with the personal motives already mentioned. It appears that the capability of expressing different emotions simultaneously makes music especially well suited to the presentation and affective resolution of ambivalence. Now from the beginning, the principal feature (not only dynamic but also formal) of the Don Juan character is a tension between unchecked sensuality and the guilt and punishment tendency. Through the suppleness and immediacy of musical expression these two elements are again unified in an artistic harmony. Thus while on the one hand the force of the musical chords announcing the Commander raises the hero's conflict of conscience to the most agonizing level, over it there soars the passionate rhythm of an unbroken conquering nature—a nature of such sensuality as we look for in vain in the whole of the vast Don Juan literature. And while the primal guilt that is released in the grieving son rages in the sounds of the Stone Guest's appearance at the banquet, there is an equally high point of sensual joy—in unbroken high spirits, Don Juan drinks "to the noble Mozart!"

---

rapher, Artur Schurig (1913) has again returned to this demoniacal feature of Mozart's personality. [This footnote, added in version C, is a close paraphrase of an article reviewing Schurig's book, "Mozart in neuem Lichte," in the *Neues Wiener Journal*, March 1, 1923, p. 4. The article is preserved in the Rank papers.]

BIBLIOGRAPHY

Almqvist, C. J. L. *Ramido Marinesco*. 1854.

Austen, J. *The story of Don Juan*. London: Martin Secker, 1939.

Bachofen, J. J. *Myth, religion, and mother right*. Selected writings. Princeton, New Jersey: Princeton University Press, 1967.

Balint, M. *Primary love and psychoanalytic technique*. Rev. ed. New York: Liveright Publishing Corporation, 1965.

Baudelaire, C. Don Juan aux enfers. [Don Juan in hell] Poem in *Les fleurs du mal*. Composed about 1843; published in 1846.

Beer, G. *Steinverehrung bei den Israeliten*. Berlin, 1921.

Bernhardi, O. C. (pseudonym of R. Zoozmann) *Don Juan*. 1903.

Bleiler, E. Translation and introduction to Da Ponte libretto of *Don Giovanni*. New York: Dover Publications, Inc., 1964.

Bowlby, J. *Attachment and loss*. Vol. 1. New York: Basic Books, 1969.

Byron, George Gordon, Lord. *Don Juan*. 1819-24.

Consten, H. *Weideplätze der Mongolen im Reiche der Chalcha*. 2 Vol. Berlin: Dietrich Reimer Verlag, 1919.

Daudet, L. *L'Hérédo. Essai sur le drame intérieur*. Paris: Nouvelle Librarie Nationale, 1916.

Dorimon. *Le festin de pierre, ou le fils criminel*. 1659.

Dumas *père*, A. *Don Juan de Maraña; ou la chute d'un ange*. 1836.

Ellinger, G. Introduction to E.T.A. Hoffman, *Werke*,

Auf Grund der Hempelschen Ausgabe neu heraus-gegeben. 5 Vol. Berlin: Deutsches Verlaghaus Borg & Co., 1912. (See the "Lebensbild," Vol. 1, pp. vii-cxxviii.)

Engels, F. *The origin of the family, private property and the state.* 1884. New York: International Publishers, 1972.

Ewald, W. Gedanken über ein Buch. *Das litterarische Echo,* 1922, *24,* 12, columns 727-30.

Fairbairn, W.R.D. *Psychoanalytic studies of the personality.* London: Routledge & Kegan Paul, Ltd., 1952.

Farinelli, A. Don Giovanni: note critiche. *Giornale storico della letteratura Italiana,* 1896, *26,* 1-77, 254-326. (Also published as a book in 1896.)

Fenichel, O. *The psychoanalytic theory of neurosis.* New York: W. W. Norton & Company, Inc., 1945.

Ferenczi, S., and Rank, O. *Entwicklungsziele der Psychoanalyse.* [Developmental aims of psychoanalysis] Leipzig, Vienna, and Zurich: Internationaler Psychoanalytischer Verlag, 1924. Translated by C. Newton as *The development of psychoanalysis.* New York and Washington: Nervous and Mental Diseases Publishing Company, 1925.

Freud, S. *The interpretation of dreams.* 2nd edition. 1909. In *Standard edition of the complete psychological works of Sigmund Freud,* Vol. 4-5. London: The Hogarth Press, 1953-57.

———. *Leonardo da Vinci and a memory of his childhood.* 1910. (a) In *Standard edition,* Vol. 11.

———. A special type of choice of object made by men. 1910. (b) In *Standard edition,* Vol. 11, pp. 163-75.

————. *Totem and taboo.* 1913. In *Standard edition,* Vol. 13.

————. On the history of the psychoanalytic movement. 1914. (a) In *Standard edition,* Vol. 14, pp. 3-66.

————. On narcissism: an introduction. 1914. (b) In *Standard edition,* Vol. 14, pp. 67-102.

————. Some character types met with in psychoanalytic work. 1916. In *Standard edition,* Vol. 14, pp. 309-33.

————. *Group psychology and the analysis of the ego.* 1921. In *Standard edition,* Vol. 18.

Friedmann, A. *Don Juans letztes Abenteuer.* [Don Juan's last adventure] 1881.

Frobenius, L. *Das Zeitalter des Sonnengottes I.* Berlin: Druck und Verlag von Georg Reiner, 1904.

Gautier, T. *La comédie de la mort.* [The comedy of death] 1838.

Gazzaniga, G. *Il convitato di pietra.* [The stone guest] 1787.

Gobineau, A., comte de. *Les adieux de Don Juan.* [Don Juan's farewell] 1844.

Grabbe, C. D. *Don Juan und Faust.* 1829.

Granero, J. M., S.J. *Don Miguel Mañara Leca y Colona y Vicentelo: estudio biográfico.* Seville: Artes Gráficas Salesianas, 1961.

Grimm, J.L.C., and Grimm, W. C. *Kinder- und Hausmärchen.* Göttingen: Druck und Verlag der Dieterichischen Buchhandlung, 1837.

Guerra Junqueiro. *A morte de Don João.* [Don Juan's death] 1874.

Guntrip, H. *Personality structure and human interaction.* New York: International Universities Press, Inc., 1961

Hart, J. *Don Juan Tenorio*. 1881.

Heckel, H. *Das Don Juan-Problem in der neueren Dichtung*. [The Don Juan problem in modern poetry] Stuttgart: J. B. Metzlersche Buchhandlung GmbH, 1915.

Heidel, A. *The Babylonian Genesis*. 2nd ed. Chicago: University of Chicago Press, 1951.

Hertel, J. (Ed.) *Indische Märchen*. Jena: Verlag bei Eugen Diederichs, 1921.

Heyse, P. *Don Juans Ende*. [Don Juan's end] 1883.

Hirsch, J. Über traditionellen Speisenabscheu. *Zeitschrift für Psychologie*, 1922, *88*, 337-71.

Hoffman, E.T.A. Don Juan: eine fabelhafte Begebenheit. Story published in 1813; later published in *Tales from Hoffman*.

Holtei, K. von. *Don Juan*. 1834.

Hunt, M. Translation of *Grimm's fairy tales*. New York: Pantheon Books, 1944.

Jekels, L. Shakespeares Macbeth. *Imago*, 1917, *5*, 170-95.

Jones, E. *The life and work of Sigmund Freud*. 3 Vols. London: Hogarth Press, 1955-57.

Jones, J. Otto Rank. In *International encyclopedia of the social sciences*, Vol. 13, pp. 314-18. New York: The Macmillan Company & the Free Press, 1968.

Jung, C. G. Psychological aspects of the mother archetype. 1938. In *Collected works of C. G. Jung*, Vol. 9, part I. 2nd ed. Princeton, New Jersey: Princeton University Press, 1969.

Kaplan, L. The psychology of literary invention. *Psyche and Eros*, 1921, *2*, 65-80.

Karpf, F. *The psychology and psychotherapy of Otto Rank*. New York: Philosophical Library, 1953.

Kierkegaard, S. The immediate stages of the erotic. 1843.

In *Either/Or*, Vol. 1, pp. 35-110. Princeton, New Jersey: Princeton University Press, 1944.

Klein, M., and Riviere, J. *Love, hate and reparation.* 1937. New York: W. W. Norton & Company, Inc., 1964.

Kleinpaul, R. *Die Lebendigen und die Toten in Volksglauben, Religion und Sage.* [The living and the dead in popular belief, religion and legend] Leipzig: G. J. Gosschen'sche Verhandlung, 1898.

Koty, J. *Die Behandlung der Alten und Kranken bei den Naturvölkern.* [The treatment of the aged and sick among primitive peoples] Stuttgart: Verlag von C. L. Hirschfeld, 1934.

Kralik, R., and Winter, J. *Deutsche Puppenspiele.* [German puppet plays] Vienna: Verlag von Carlo Konegen, 1885.

Krause, F.E.A. Die Familienorganisation als Grundlage des privaten und öffentlichen Lebens in China. [The family organization as the basis of private and public life in China] *Deutsche Revue,* 1922, 47, 1, 156-65 and 257-69.

Kretschmer, P. (Ed.) *Neugriekische Märchen.* Jena: Verlag bei Eugen Diederichs, 1917.

Kroeber, A. L. *Totem and taboo* in retrospect. *American Journal of Sociology,* 1939, 45, 446-51.

Lavedan, H. *Le marquis de Priola.* 1902.

Lenau, N. *Don Juan.* 1851.

Leskien, A. (Ed.) *Balkanmärchen aus Albanien, Bulgarien, Serbian und Kroatien.* Jena: Verlag bei Eugen Diederichs, 1919.

Levavasseur, G. *Don Juan Barbon.* 1848.

MacKay, D. E. *The double invitation in the legend of Don Juan.* Stanford, California: Stanford University Press, 1943.

Maddi, S. R. *Personality theories: a comparative analysis.*
Rev. ed. Homewood, Illinois: Dorsey Press, 1972.
Maeztu, R. de. Don Juan o el poder. In *Don Quixote,*
Don Juan y la Celestina. Madrid: Espasa-Calpe,
1938.
Mallefille, J.P.F. *Mémoirs de Don Juan.* 1852.
Mandel, O. (Ed.) *The theatre of Don Juan.* Lincoln,
Nebraska: University of Nebraska Press, 1963.
Marañón, G. *Don Juan.* Madrid: Espasa-Calpe, 1940.
Mérimée, P. *Les Âmes du purgatoire. Nouvelle.* [The
ghosts of purgatory] 1834.
Molière (pseudonym of J. P. Poquelin). *Don Juan ou le*
festin de pierre. [Don Juan or the stone guest] 1665.
Mozart, W. A. *Il dissoluto punito, ossia il Don Giovanni.*
Libretto by L. Da Ponte. 1787.
Müller-Fraureuth, C. *Die deutschen Lügendichtungen*
bis auf Münchhausen. Halle: Max Niemeyer, 1881.
Munroe, R. L. *Schools of psychoanalytic thought.* New
York: Dryden Press, 1955.
Musset, A. de. *Namouna.* 1832.
Naumann, H. *Primitive Gemeinschaftskultur.* Jena: Ver-
lag bei Eugen Diederichs, 1921.
Nin, A. *The diary of Anaïs Nin.* 4 Vols. New York:
Harcourt, Brace & World, Inc., 1966-67.
Nunberg, H., and Federn, E. (Eds.) *Minutes of the*
Vienna Psychoanalytic Society. Vol. 1. New York:
International Universities Press, 1962.
Poppe, N. Geserica. Untersuchungen der sprachlichen
Eigentümlichkeiten der Mongolischen Version des
Gesserkhan. *Asia Major,* 1926, *3,* 1-32 and 167-93.
Pratt, D. The Don Juan myth. *American Imago,* 1960,
17, 321-35.
Preller, L. *Griechische Mythologie.* 4th ed. Berlin: Weid-
mannsche Buchhandlung, 1887.

Progoff, I. *The death and rebirth of psychology*. New York: The Julian Press, Inc., 1956.

Pushkin, A. S. *Kamennyi Gost*. 1830.

Rank, B. Zur Rolle der Frau in der Entwicklung der menschlichen Gesellschaft. [On the role of the woman in the development of human society] *Imago*, 1924, *10*, 278-95.

Rank, O. *Der Künstler: Ansätze zu einer Sexualpsychologie*. [The artist: approaches toward a sexual psychology] Vienna: Heller, 1907.

———. *Das Inzest-Motiv in Dichtung und Sage: Grundzüge einer Psychologie des dichterischen Schaffens*. [The incest motif in literature and legend: outline of a psychology of literary creation] Leipzig and Vienna: Deuticke, 1912.

———. Die Matrone von Ephesus: ein Deutungsversuch der Fabel von der treulosen Witwe. [The matron of Ephesus: an attempt at interpretation of the fable of the faithless widow] *Internationale Zeitschrift für ärtzliche Psychoanalyse*, 1913, *1*, 50-60.

———. Der Doppelgänger: eine psychoanalytische Studie. [The double: a psychoanalytic study] *Imago*, 1914, *3*, 97-164. English translation by H. Tucker, Jr., published 1971 by the University of North Carolina Press.

———. *Psychoanalytische Beiträge zur Mythenforschung; gesammelte Studien aus den Jahren 1912 bis 1914*. [Psychoanalytic contributions to the study of myth; collected studies from 1912-1914] Leipzig and Vienna: Internationaler Psychoanalytischer Verlag, 1919, 2nd ed., 1922.

———. Die Don Juan-Gestalt. *Imago*, 1922, *8*, 142-96.

———. Zum Verständnis der Libidoentwicklung im Heilungsvorgang: (I) Die psychische Potenz; (II)

Idealbildung und Liebeswahl. [Toward understanding libidinal development in the course of healing: (I) Psychic potency; (II) Ideal-formation and object choice] *Internationale Zeitschrift für Psychoanalyse*, 1923, *9*, 435-71.

———. *Die Don Juan-Gestalt*. Leipzig, Vienna, and Zurich: Internationaler Psychoanalytischer Verlag, 1924. (a)

———. *Das Trauma der Geburt und seine Bedeutung für die Psychoanalyse*. [The trauma of birth and its meaning for psychoanalysis] Leipzig, Vienna, and Zurich: Internationaler Psychoanalytischer Verlag, 1924. (b) English translation published 1929 by Paul, Trench, and Trübner (London) and Harcourt, Brace (New York).

———. The genesis of genitality. *Psychoanalytic Review*, 1926, *13*, 129-44.

———. Don Juan und Leporello. In *Almanach für das Jahr 1927*. Leipzig, Vienna, and Zurich: Internationaler Psychoanalytischer Verlag, 1927, pp. 172-80.

———. *Seelenglaube und Psychologie*. [The belief in souls and psychology] Leipzig and Vienna: Deuticke, 1930. English translation by W. D. Turner under the title *Psychology and the Soul* published 1950 by the University of Pennsylvania Press.

———. *Art and artist*. New York: Alfred A. Knopf, Inc., 1932. (a)

———. *Don Juan. Une étude sur le double*. Paris: Denoël & Steele, 1932. (b)

———. *Beyond psychology*. 1941. New York: Dover Publications, Inc., 1958.

Reik, T. *Psychology of sex relations*. 1945. New York: Grove Press, 1966.

Rittner, T. *Unterwegs: eine Don Juan-Drama*. 1909.

Roheim, G. Steinheiligtum und Grab. *Internationale Zeitschrift für Psychoanalyse*, 1921, 7, 523.

Rose, H. J. *A handbook of Greek mythology*. 5th ed., revised. London: Methuen & Co., Ltd., 1953.

Rostand, E. *La dernière nuit de Don Juan*. 1921.

Sachs, H. *Freud—master and friend*. Cambridge, Mass.: Harvard University Press, 1944.

Schmitz, O.A.H. *Don Juan, Casanova, und andere erotische Charaktere: ein Versuch*. [Don Juan, Casanova, and other erotic characters: a study] 2nd ed. Stuttgart: Axel Juncker Verlag, 1913.

Schoning, O. Dodsriger i Nordisk hedentro. *Studier fra Sprag- og Oldtidsforskning*, Number 57. Copenhagen: Kleins Forlag, 1903.

Schrader, P. *Totenhochzeit*. [Marriage of the dead] 1904.

Schur, M. *Freud: living and dying*. New York: International Universities Press, 1972.

Schurig, A. *Wolfgang Amadeus Mozart. Sein Leben und sein Werke*. Leipzig, 1913.

Shadwell, T. *The libertine*. 1676.

Shaw, G. B. *Man and superman*. 1903.

Singer, A. E. *The Don Juan theme, versions, and criticism: a bibliography*. Revised edition. Morgantown, West Virginia. West Virginia University Press, 1965.

Stekel, W. Masken der Homosexualität. [Masks of homosexuality] *Zentralblatt für Psychoanalyse und Psychotherapie*, 1912, 2, 367-72.

Stendhal (pseudonym of M. H. Beyle). *Vie de Mozart*. 1814. (The author claimed that this was a translation of a biographical notice by M. Schlichtegroll, but the original author is now held to be T. F. Winckler, writing in 1801.)

Stendhal. *De L'amour*. 1822.

Sternheim, C. *Don Juan*. 1909.

Taft, J. *Otto Rank: a biographical study*. New York: The Julian Press, Inc., 1958.

Thomas, P. *Epics, myths and legends of India*. Bombay: D. B. Taraporevala Sons & Co., 1961.

Tolstoi, A. K. *Don Zhuan*. 1860.

Viard, J. *La vieillesse de Don Juan*. [The aging years of Don Juan] 1853.

Villiers, C. D., sieur de. *Le festin de pierre ou le fils criminel*. 1660.

Waelder, R. *Basic theory of psychoanalysis*. New York: International Universities Press, 1960.

Wagner, R. *Mein Leben*. 2 Vol. Munich: F. Bruckmann A. G., 1911.

Weinstein, L. *The metamorphoses of Don Juan*. Stanford, Calif.: Stanford University Press, 1959.

Werner, R. M. *Der Laufner Don Juan*. Hamburg and Leipzig: Verlag von Leopold Voss, 1891.

Wilhelm, R. (Ed.) *Chinesische Volksmärchen*. Jena: Verlag bei Eugen Diederichs, 1914.

Winter, D. G. *The power motive*. New York: The Free Press, 1973.

Worthington, M. Don Juan as myth. *Literature and psychology*, 1962, *12*, 113-24.

Zorilla y Moral, J. *Don Juan Tenorio*. 1844.

INDEX

Abraham, K., 11, 13-14
Almqvist, C. J. L., 111, 127
Amphitryon motif, 59, 110-111
anaclitic attachment, different
    motives of mother and son,
    93-94
animals: appropriation of
    strength of by eating, 79;
    Cerberus, 70; death and,
    69-71; vulture, 69, 71
animism, primitive, 65, 98;
    neurosis and, 80
anxiety about the return of the
    dead, 64, 65; caused by
    Oedipus complex, 65;
    checked by destruction of
    corpse, 64-65, 79; Don Juan
    succumbs to, 87; reworked
    into a mirthful banquet,
    76, 87
Arndt, A., 51n
art: analysis of content of,
    44; development of, 108,
    109; form, 44; functions of,
    120-122; psychology
    (psychoanalysis) and, 41-42,
    49, 97, 107, 108-109, 120.
    See also Rank, Otto,
    changing views on psycho-
    analytic interpretation and
    art
artist (poet): anti-social,
    121-122; converges with
    "hero" type, 122; devalues
    subject in later "periods" of

work, 24, 30, 106, 107, 111,
    116-117, 119, 120-121; dis-
    appointment and failure of,
    24, 122-123; distorts primal
    deed in "heroic" stage, 21,
    24, 55, 82, 88, 106; fantasies
    and motives of arise out of
    guilt, 105-106, 109, 120;
    interpretation (elucidation)
    by, 57, 97, 106, 107, 120;
    moral sense of, 122;
    narcissism of, 24, 121-123;
    "periods" in the work of,
    123-124; Rank's theories
    about, 32-34; repeats the
    primal crime, 121; social
    function of, 23-24, 30,
    120-122
audience, reaction of to
    Don Juan, 38
Austen, J., 22n, 40n, 127

Bachofen, J. J., 92n, 127
Balint, M., 23, 127
Balzac, H. de, 50, 51n
banquet (Don Juan and
    statue), 47, 48, 52, 76, 106,
    114, 126
Baudelaire, C., 115, 127
Beer, G., 75, 127
Bernhardi, O. C., 29, 116, 127
Bogda Gesser Chan, 85
Bowlby, J., 23, 127
Brothers, Band of, 55, 110-111;
    Amphitryon motif and, 111;

137

139

140

Library of Congress Cataloging in Publication Data

Rank, Otto, 1884-1939.
  The Don Juan legend.

  Translation of Die Don-Juan Gestalt.
  Bibliography: p.
  Includes index.
  1. Psychoanalysis. 2. Juan, Don. I. Title.
  BF175.R313   150'.19'5   72-6528
  ISBN 0-691-08605-2

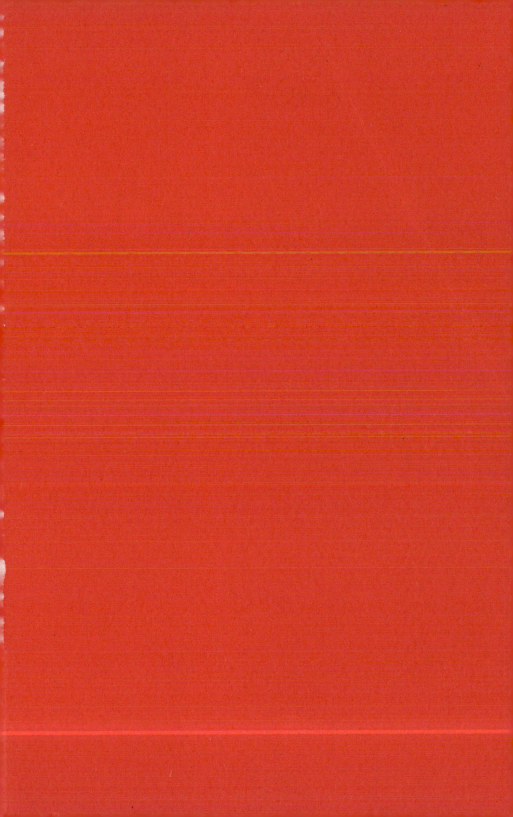